W9-CEZ-569

Public Relations for Librarians

Public Relations for Librarians

K. C. Harrison

Grafton Basic Texts
Editor: Evelyn J. A. Evans, CBE, FLA

ANDRE DEUTSCH/A Grafton Book

First published 1973 by
André Deutsch Limited
105 Great Russell Street London WC1

Printed in Great Britain by
Ebenezer Baylis & Son Ltd
The Trinity Press, Worcester, and London

ISBN 0 233 95657 3

The opinions expressed in this book
are those of the author writing in a
personal capacity and are not necessarily
those of his employing authority

Contents

1. Libraries and the outside world   9
2. The PR value of personal service   23
3. Librarians as print-users   30
4. Relations with press, radio, TV and other media   41
5. Co-operative library publicity   54
6. Oral library publicity   73
7. Exhibitions, display work and other activities   84
8. The future of library promotion   95

Select bibliography   103
Index   107

List of Plates

Between pages 16 and 17

Ten-year souvenir brochure of the Amerika Gedenkbibliothek.

Front cover of a brochure published by the Deutsche Bücherei, Leipzig.

Front cover of Luton Library's two-yearly report.

Front cover of the handbook for Britain's second National Library Week in 1967.

Front cover of a brochure from Skövde, Sweden.

Between pages 48 and 49

Poster for Britain's first National Library Week.

Two National Library Week bookmarks.

Cover of a four-page leaflet from the Enoch Pratt Free Library, Baltimore.

Cover of the twelve-sided folder from the Clements Library at the University of Michigan, Ann Arbor.

Between pages 80 and 81

Front cover of Stockholm City Library's folder about children's services.

Folder issued by Minneapolis Public Library and Hennepin County Library.

List of Plates

Two-fold leaflet from the public library at Santa Monica (California).

Examples of postcards as PR material from Gothenberg City Libraries.

Anniversary booklists: 'Charles Dickens 1812–1870' and '50 years of the BBC'.

Chapter 1
Libraries and the outside world

When librarians think of public relations in a superficial manner – and we too often think superficially on this topic – it is nearly always considered in the simple light of relations between librarians and users, or potential users. But this is an over-simplification of the problem. Of course it is true that the ultimate objective of library public relations is to ensure that the maximum number of people know of the existence of our libraries, where they are located, what they contain, and how they can help users to acquire more information and generally become more literate and better educated members of the community. Yet any public relations programme which begins and ends by concentrating solely upon readers and other library users can never hope to be more than a partial success.

The fact is that libraries, if they are to continue to develop, must be projected in many ways and in many directions, and not merely to individual readers or groups of potential users. They must be projected internationally, nationally, regionally, locally, and sectionally with such related activities as central government, education, local government, vocational training, the social services, the book trade, and not forgetting library staffs themselves.

It is perhaps not until one becomes a senior librarian that realization comes of the vital importance of this aspect of public relations for libraries vis-a-vis the outside world. As a junior member of the profession it is all too easy to confine library public relations in the mind to a programme concerned only with users. But as one gains more professional experience, the wider aspects of PR for libraries become more obvious and important. Perhaps it is only when one becomes a chief librarian or a director of libraries that the fullest appreciation of PR and its range and influence is attained.

9

The good chief librarian, like the good military commander in the field, should not become too bogged down in administrative detail. He should have time to sit down and to plan broad lines of strategy and development, and to do this effectively he ought to be capable of seeing his library service in its international, national and regional roles, as well as in its purely local context.

Sitting back, however, does not mean becoming office-bound. On the contrary, the director ought to play his part in the activities of international and national library associations, for only in this way will he have the opportunities of watching and keeping abreast of library development throughout the world. Locally, the director must be the 'front man' for his library. His governing body, and his public, must be able to turn to him with confidence whenever the topics of libraries, books and other information media crop up. He must be able to write and to speak fluently on behalf of his calling, and nowhere will this fluency be more taxed, or more important, than in the committee rooms of his governing authority.

Perhaps the most important aspect of the work of a director of libraries is to persuade his governing body to supply enough money for the efficient operation and development of the service. Good operation, or day-to-day running of libraries, cannot properly be maintained without a healthy revenue budget. Each year, therefore, or however frequently the authority plans its revenue budgeting, it is necessary for the director to prepare detailed estimates and to pilot them through his board or committee. Development calls for more long-term thinking, and the preparation of a capital budgeting programme looking several years ahead. Vision is therefore a most essential commodity in the personality of a director of libraries.

A good library is, or should be, its own advertisement, and it should not be necessary to have to persuade authorities to devote adequate finances for library buildings, staff, books and related materials. Unfortunately it is necessary, and in this exercise of persuasion it is a proven fact that a director who can write a compelling report, and can speak on it convincingly, is much more likely to be successful than one who presents an incomplete report, speaks confusedly on it, and answers questions in an unconvincing manner. It may be wrong that important public issues should be decided against such backgrounds, but it is one of the facts of life that sometimes happens.

This theme will be developed later, but it is important to make the point as soon as possible that the most vital factor in a good PR programme for libraries is an efficient, energetic and knowledgeable director with an astute appreciation of the value of PR in its widest applications.

LIBRARIES AND GOVERNMENTS

Almost every type of library, apart from special and industrial libraries and privately owned collections, stem in some way from the powers of national governments. In most countries public libraries derive their existence and development from government. So, of course, do national libraries, as well as university, college and school libraries. In addition, most governments are themselves considerable owners of libraries, be they national, legislative or departmental in scope. How vitally important it is therefore to ensure that members of governments are adequately briefed about the scope and objectives of libraries of all kinds!

Before discussing government orientated PR programmes for libraries, let us touch briefly on international aspects. The comparative approach can be very influential, since governments of all countries are capable of being influenced by what is happening in other countries. In no field has this been better demonstrated than in that of library and information science, and such bodies as Unesco, the International Federation of Library Associations, and the Féderation Internationale de Documentation have achieved profitable results for international progress in the field over the last thirty years. This has been done mainly by demonstrating to the less well-developed library countries the good effects upon literacy and education noticed in such areas as the USA, Britain and Scandinavia, which possess established, though by no means perfect, library and information science complexes.

Unesco has been a major influence for good through its pilot projects in such countries as India and Colombia, through its programme of sending experienced library consultants to developing countries, through its fellowship scheme which enables librarians from developing countries to visit established libraries in other parts of the world, and not least through the medium of the *Unesco Bulletin for Libraries*, circulated throughout the world in four languages, English, French, Spanish and Russian.

The International Federation of Library Associations (IFLA) has influenced library progress in a different way, but mainly through the annual meetings of its Council and a proliferation of committees studying and reporting upon most facets of library science. Its journal *Libri* has also been a power for good. The Féderation Internationale de Documentation (FID) has done, and is still doing, similar good work to spread throughout the world the latest developments in documentation and information science, again chiefly through its meetings and its publications.

Unesco, IFLA and FID all lean heavily upon the good will and financial support of governments, but they must also rely on support from national library associations. Most national library associations do in fact support international development, but to varying degrees. Would that more of them gave support in the way in which the American Library Association did! This body had the foresight to set up an International Relations Division, situated in Washington, DC, deliberately close to the corridors of power. This Division handled all international affairs for ALA, whether it was arranging consultancies for countries overseas, organizing programmes for visitors, arranging conferences, and conducting international library correspondence on behalf of its parent association. Unfortunately, ALA has for financial reasons had to close this Division.

I mention this in a book on PR simply because it was a good and welcome PR activity. It may be true that basically the ALA's International Relations Division was promoting American library expertise, but there is nothing to stop other national library associations from carrying out similar activities. In Britain, the Library Association has been urged to set up a parallel Division, but lack of adequate finance has so far prevented this. However, British librarians should not assume that the LA is not active internationally, since a great deal has been accomplished without benefit of a separate International Relations Division or committee. Participation in international conferences, the establishment of internships for overseas librarians in British libraries, the arrangement of programmes for visiting librarians, publications of an international character, all these and other activities have been and are being efficiently carried out by the LA.

The British Council also has a good international record in librarianship. Although its libraries overseas have been reduced in number and an increase in them is urgently needed, it continues to arrange many courses for visiting librarians to Britain, and it also sends British librarians abroad either as consultants or visitors. Co-operation between the British Council, the LA, and individual library authorities in Britain is maintained on a very close basis.

Another recent development for good public relations in the international library field has been the establishment of the Commonwealth Library Association. Following a suggestion from the Commonwealth Foundation, which has funded the initial steps, all the library associations in the Commonwealth agreed to take part, and COMLA, as it is known, was set up in 1972. This can only lead to closer co-operation, to a greater knowledge of mutual problems and solutions, and to more possibilities of promoting libraries in the countries of the Commonwealth.

World library development through international agencies presumes an interest in and knowledge of comparative librarianship on the part of all national library associations. But all associations are comprised of individuals, so it is at individual level that interest in comparative librarianship and in positive public relations must be engendered and encouraged.

Leaving the international scene we now arrive at national level to look at the problems of acquainting governments and legislators with a comprehensive and up-to-date appreciation of libraries. We have already seen that governments are the owners of many national and departmental libraries, and they largely finance the activities of many others, including university and other libraries associated with education. In many countries governments also give direct or indirect financial aid towards the maintenance and development of public libraries. So it is vital that ministers, members of legislative bodies, and senior civil servants should be properly briefed on the subject.

Some countries, notably those in Scandinavia, have state library offices to advise their governments on library development. In Britain, since the latest public library law became operative in 1965, we have had Library Advisory Councils, and now there is a Libraries and Arts Branch of the Department of Education and Science to advise the appropriate responsible Minister. But the existence of these arrangements should never absolve either library associations or individual librarians from acting as watchdogs on behalf of the profession. Every opportunity must be taken to give evidence to commissions whose investigations touch in any way upon libraries. Neither should the practice of lobbying members of legislative bodies be overlooked. It is perhaps an unfortunate necessity, but it is an accepted way of modern political life. Most professions have their lobbies in the main political parties, and librarianship cannot afford to be left out.

There are many ways in which individual members of the profession can help in getting view points over to those responsible for ruling the country. One is by writing to one's Member of Parliament whenever matters affecting libraries are due for discussion. It is an undoubted fact that American librarians write to their Congressmen and Senators much more frequently than British librarians write to their Members of Parliament. A recent cause for concern in the United States has been the topic of intellectual freedom, and it is encouraging to know that American librarians have not been slow to defend this by writing letters to their representatives in Congress and Senate on the subject.

There should be no feelings of compunction about this. If the intention is not to pressurize but to inform our legislators of the way we experts feel, then the writing of such letters is quite unexceptionable. How, after all, can legislators arrive at proper conclusions if they have not considered the fullest expert advice from all quarters?

Some librarians feel that lobbying and letter-writing is useless when a government has apparently made up its mind, but this has proved wrong on numerous occasions. When the British Government decided in 1966 not to allow the southern expansion of the British Museum Library there was a great outcry, not only from the Trustees of the Library, but also from the Library Association and many other academic bodies, and from individuals including educationists, librarians and the general public. The result of this activity, which included letter-writing to the press and lobbying of Members of Parliament, was that the Government changed its mind and the British Museum Library will, later in the 1970s, be able to expand in the desired direction.

There will, in the future, be many proposals in many countries of the world, which will require watchdog activity of this kind on the part of librarians and their friends in other professions. Financial stringencies which unfairly affect libraries may need to be opposed. The question of the Public Lending Right in the United Kingdom might have been a *fait accompli* by this time had it not been for the reactions of the local authority associations, local authorities themselves, the Library Association, and many individual librarians, all giving powerful reasons why PLR was unacceptable in the original forms in which it was proposed. Another, and more urgent question in Britain, may be a proposal to make charges to readers for the borrowing of books from public libraries. If such a proposal ever came before Parliament, it would need to be opposed as vigorously as possible, and this would involve the briefing of Members of Parliament and the application of the maximum public relations skill that can be mustered by the library profession.

PR AND LIBRARY GOVERNING BODIES

It is incredible, but one of the major failures of librarians in the past has been in the matter of communication between them and members of their own governing bodies. Surely it should be a first essential for any librarian to keep his governing body fully and effectively informed on all aspects of his library's services, achievements and developments. He has various means at his disposal for maintaining this necessary communication.

The first is by regular written reports to his board or committee, but it must always be borne in mind that the presentation of such reports can make or mar the communication between officers and members. There has been a tendency in the past for officers to produce too many written reports, but this has been checked in many countries, and especially in the United Kingdom by the publication of the Maud and the Mallaby Reports on local government organization and staffing. The combined effects of these Reports have been to widen the powers of chief officers, with the tendency to confine the contents of committee agendas to matters of policy. This means fewer written reports, but those which are presented are necessarily of importance, and it is vital that they should be well-written and well-presented.

The elements of a good report are fairness of presentation, clarity and brevity – and the greatest of these is brevity. Members of governing bodies are busy men and women, and it is not unnatural that they become impatient when they have to cope with many lengthy, complex and verbose reports. Granted that good report-writing is a fine art which may not be commanded by everybody, but it is perfectly possible to present members with all the facts fairly, clearly, briefly and often with a straightforward and uncomplicated recommendation. Prime Minister Winston Churchill was not being unreasonable when he asked that reports to him should be confined to one side of a sheet of foolscap. Now that international paper sizes are used, foolscap has disappeared in favour of the slightly smaller A4 size, so it should now be the aim of directors of libraries to confine their committee reports to one side of a sheet of A4.

Of course it is not always possible to do this, or even desirable if the matter under report is of signal importance, but I am sure the point is taken by readers.

To aid in brevity there should be little need for adjectives

The Amerika Gedenkbibliothek in West Berlin used an attractive photographic setting of its distinctive building for the front cover of its ten-year souvenir brochure.

Typographic repetition combined with photographs in colour forms the front cover of a 70-page brochure published by the Deutsche Bücherei in Leipzig. Inside there are many illustrations, and the text is in German, Russian, English and French.

LUTON PUBLIC LIBRARIES
Report for the years 1970–1972

- END OF A DECADE
- FACTS AND FIGURES
- SPOTLIGHT —
  The Information Departments
- AT RANDOM
  Books and People

For its two-yearly report Luton uses a setting of its main library in the busy heart of the town. Eight other photographs inside demonstrate various activities of the library.

The front cover of the handbook produced by the Joint
Organising Committee for Britain's second National
Library Week in 1967 contains the NLW symbol and
slogan. This introduced a sixty-page booklet, illustrated
with photographs and cartoons, and giving all possible
information and guidance to local organisers.

Skövde in Sweden uses the family approach in this colour photograph forming the front
cover of this brochure, which also contains eleven other pictures of the library
departments, a plan of the library lay-out, and an outline key to the classification used.

and adverbs. George Rylands, the lecturer and literary critic whose studies of Shakespeare are so perceptive, once said that no adjective is above suspicion. Although he was writing about words and poetry, his comment applies equally to prose, and he might have included adverbs as well.

So keep your reports brief, clear and unadorned. Paragraphs should be kept short and should be serially numbered for ease of reference. A summing-up paragraph at the end should lead to a clear recommendation, with reasons given if thought necessary.

The reports referred to are, of course, confidential ones not normally for public consumption. The librarian's annual report comes into a different category. It can be made into a major PR document for the library, affording communication between the librarian and his governing body, and between the librarian and his users, or his potential users. As most annual reports are, or should be, printed and published, further comment on its presentation and production is deferred to a subsequent chapter devoted to printed library publicity.

Personal relations between the librarian and members of his council and board are extremely important, but especially so between the librarian and his chairman. The chairman of the governing body of the library should be a key figure in the library's progress, since he is the person who has to explain and interpret its policy and needs to those who ultimately control the purse-strings. He cannot do this effectively if he is not fully informed, and it is the librarian's job to keep in constant close touch with his chairman and to brief him as fully as possible.

This is not an easy task. The chairman, when wanted, may be unavailable. Then, when you do see or speak to him, you may inadvertently forget a salient point you wished to make. Selection of information is important too. The chairman often needs to have a certain amount of detail without being overloaded with trivia. What the librarian should try to do is to put himself in the position of the chairman, and satisfy himself in this way that the latter is in possession of all the relevant information.

LIBRARIES AND THE BOOK TRADE

Time was when libraries apparently operated in isolation so far as the rest of the book world was concerned, but this was never really the whole truth and in recent years it has become increasingly apparent that the librarian is just one cog, though a vital one, in a wheel which also includes the author, the publisher, the bookseller and the reader. So here again a PR exercise on behalf of libraries is necessary if our co-producers of the information media are fully to appreciate our problems and objectives.

Booksellers need to know the urgent needs of libraries to supply their readers with books as quickly as possible, and of our requirements in the way of accurate invoicing. Publishers may seek our opinions on gaps in the subject provision of books, or on library editions, or on out-of-print books. A lot of this interplay and exchange of opinion can and should be done between the various national associations, but individual librarians must play their parts as well.

The growth of National Library Weeks and similar co-operative ventures in the USA, the UK, Denmark, Canada, Australia and other countries has undoubtedly improved the collaboration between libraries and other sections of the book world, and I will be enlarging upon this in a later chapter on co-operative library publicity. Meanwhile, much remains to be done to cement this growing contact. Obviously the author, the bookseller, the librarian and the publisher are all different components of the book world, each having differing aims. It is not to be expected that we shall agree on everything all the time but – and this cannot be repeated too often – we are all relatively small sections of the community at large, and we can achieve much more by working together as much as possible than we can ever hope to do by remaining apart in a watertight way.

Our basic aim is the common one of working to improve the literacy and the general educational and cultural level of the community. This is too important to be interrupted by petty sectional differences, but unless the PR programmes of all the bodies concerned is improved there remains the likelihood that we shall remain apart, instead of drawing closer together.

LIBRARIES AND EDUCATIONISTS

One would hardly expect educationists to be included among the enemies of libraries, but instances have happened, as most librarians would agree. Only a small minority of educationists have fallen into this category, but they have existed, and still exist. There can only be one reason, and that surely must lie in the ineffective PR programmes of librarians.

Happily this situation is improving. Most new universities have started from the premise that the library is the first and basic requirement of the institution. The development of college and school libraries continues, and co-operation between lecturers, teachers and librarians gets slowly closer to the desired ideal.

Librarians and library associations cannot, however, afford to relax their PR efforts in the direction of formal education, for there are still vice-chancellors who appear reluctant to grant the university library its proper place, there are still education officers and committees who are satisfied with sub-standard school libraries, and there are still headteachers who do not fully appreciate the value of public library services to the children under their care.

Only a constant and carefully planned PR programme will improve these situations. One thing, however, must be under-lined. Of all sections of the community those concerned with education are perhaps the quickest to appreciate a good library service when they experience it. The moral then should be that when librarians are serving educationists they should gear themselves to produce the best possible service.

INTERNAL PR

Although this chapter deals primarily with libraries and the world outside them, it ends on an internal note with some remarks about communication between the librarian and his staff, largely because this is a topic which is basic to the whole of this book. Unfortunately this aspect of communication is something which many librarians tend to overlook. Adequate arrangements are often made for staff training and welfare, but never a thought is given to keeping staffs informed about the progress of the library as a whole, or about the short-term and long-term intentions of the library authority.

We live in an era of mergers in almost every walk of life, and library services are affected as much as other activities. 'Fewer, larger and more viable' is the phrase of the moment, and as far as libraries are concerned this means larger staffs spread over wider areas. In turn, this increases the need for better communication between the director and the many members of his staff, but how many directors can put their hands on their hearts and say with certainty that they are satisfied with the level of contact between themselves and their staffs? To get a more realistic picture of the situation, one should perhaps ask the staffs what they feel about the flow (or otherwise) of information coming to them from the top echelon. Many senior librarians would get a rude shock if this were done!

This problem of communication with staff is one which may never satisfactorily be solved, but much can be done to ameliorate the situation. The director may have meetings with his senior staff, and the question arises as to whether these should be on a regular basis or should they be held as and when thought necessary? I am personally against regular meetings after discovering a tendency for senior librarians to invent items for discussion if they had nothing of an urgent nature to bring up. It is much better to arrange such meetings whenever they are deemed essential, with the proviso that a minimum number of meetings should be held each year. Another point to be stressed is that each senior librarian who attends a director's meeting should hold a meeting of his own subordinates soon afterwards. It is of no value to staff communication if the information gleaned from a director's meeting is not passed quickly down the line.

Another good medium of communication for large library staffs is the regular issue of a news-letter from the director, and ideally this should be distributed on an individual basis so that every member of the staff is given a personal copy. Not enough libraries do this, but there are some notable examples. Toledo Public Libraries, in the United States, for some years produced a chatty news-letter, written in journalistic style and complete with line-drawings. Some critics would say this lacked dignity, but it was probably read by the recipients more avidly than a more strait-laced production might have been.

There are examples of staff news-letters in the United Kingdom as well. Cheshire County Libraries and the North Riding County Libraries may be quoted: both aim to keep their far-flung staffs as fully informed as practicable on future new buildings, the progress of libraries under construction, intended developments generally, and news of past and present staff. These productions are more sober than the Toledo news-letter yet they are still well-presented and readable. In Sweden, Stockholm City Libraries have a part-time public relations librarian, part of whose duties include reporting to the staff journal. Writing in the *Scandinavian Public Library Quarterly*, vol. 3, 1, 1970, Greta Renborg said: 'If the public relations librarian were employed full-time and had an assistant, the editing of this magazine would be part of her duties. As it is at present, another staff officer handles the journal in close collaboration with the public relations librarian.'

Differentiation should be made here between the staff newsletter produced under the aegis of the director, which is the kind of publication I have been writing about, and the staff journal which is sometimes produced by the personnel themselves as the organ of the staff association. Examples occur showing that these two types of publication can be combined into one, but it is preferable that the staff association should run its own publication, leaving the director of libraries with the responsibility of producing a regular medium of communication between himself and his personnel.

Mention has just been made of Stockholm and its public relations librarian and it leads us to end this chapter by posing a question. Should large libraries employ a PR librarian or should they utilise a PR officer? There is a distinction, as the observant reader will have noticed. Stockholm is not the only large library to employ a public relations librarian, other examples coming to mind in Holland, the United Kingdom, Canada and the United States. Excellent work has been achieved by these professional librarians who have obviously acquired a modicum of PR expertise, but PR is now a profession in its own right, and would it not be better to employ a PR officer either full-time or part-time, or to utilise the services of the PRO of the local authority or the university, or even to hand out PR responsibilities to an outside firm of experts?

In the USA many libraries already employ people specially trained in PR work, Seattle Public Libraries being a case in point. Indeed, in the United States it is generally accepted that whenever possible the PR officer is to be preferred to the PR librarian. There is no doubt in my mind that when a library service reaches a certain size it should employ its own PR personnel, but that this should include a trained PRO rather than a trained librarian turned PRO.

It will frequently be found that the governing body of the library will not agree to the library having its own PRO, because it already has a section with trained PR people to cope with all aspects of the authority's activities. A great deal of useful publicity can be gained for the library by the trained PRO, because he has contacts with press, TV and radio which the library could never hope to equal. One disadvantage of this arrangement is that such an officer is concerned with so many other services that he can give only a small proportion of his time to the library's PR needs. In these circumstances, it still remains for the director of libraries and his senior staff to be aware of all publicity possibilities and to acquaint the authority's PRO with library news and developments on a regular basis.

Chapter 2
The P R value of personal service

Good wine needs no bush, and a library which offers a comprehensive, efficient and prompt service is its own best recommendation. This is a theme which may recur frequently in this book, but I make no apology for the repetition, because it needs stating and re-stating. Nevertheless, it has to be admitted that the word-of-mouth recommendation from a satisfied reader to a potential one is a slow process, and that is why libraries must consider a positive PR policy to supplement the more passive person to person recommendation.

Before we consider the more blatant and obvious PR methods, as we shall be doing in later chapters, there are some basic points to consider regarding the library's internal arrangements. First, it is essential for the librarian carefully to consider what he is offering his public, to try to define the shortcomings of his service, and to decide upon what aspects he should base his campaign. Faith in one's product is a necessity of PR campaigning, and one must be absolutely certain of being able to produce the goods before shouting their qualities from high heaven. No library service is perfect, but most have some qualities of which they can be justifiably proud. One library system may be blessed with attractive modern buildings; another may be cursed with antiquated, inadequate buildings yet may still be rich in special collections; a third might have an excellent, well-trained cadre of readers' advisers who daily bring credit to the service; a fourth may be strong in special services, such as reference and information work, or services to children and youth.

Always reinforce success, never reinforce failure, goes the military maxim, and it is one that should be followed in library PR work as well. In short, concentrate upon publicizing the aspects of your service which you believe to be good, and improve the shortcomings of other aspects before you even begin to think of publicizing them.

Another basic requirement is to organize the staff for personal service, the kind of personal service that will be required if, as is surely hoped, more readers come to use the library as a result of a PR campaign. The librarian should assure himself that he has enough staff to cope with increased demands, and especially that he has sufficient personnel to staff all the desks at which new users will present themselves. This particularly applies to readers' advisers, who should be trained and qualified, capable of exploiting the resources of the library system as a whole on behalf of enquiring readers.

The basic training of library staff is indeed an important factor in maintaining the good public image of the library. Personal appearance, neat dress and courtesy all combine to give readers a good impression of libraries and their staffs, and these traits should be cultivated and encouraged. Perhaps one of the best ways to do this is to produce a staff handbook which can be handed to new personnel when they join the service. Such a handbook may contain a great deal of basic information covering service conditions, the scope of the library and its place within the community, but also it can and should include some tactful suggestions about personal dress and appearance, as well as the importance of treating all library users with equal courtesy at all times.

Librarians and their staffs can learn much from the outside world in these matters. Observe and compare the treatment you get from the staff of a good bank, a good hotel, a good airline, a good department store, with what happens when you use bad examples of these establishments. Then ask yourself – what happens to readers in my library? Are they greeted in a clean, attractive building by a keen, personable and well-groomed staff? Are their inquiries dealt with at the right level, or do unqualified personnel try vainly to wrestle with abstruse subject inquiries, leaving behind unsatisfied users? Are patrons made restive by having sometimes to wait unnecessarily in queues? In short, is there a general un-businesslike air about your library? If these and other questions cannot in all honesty be answered satisfactorily by the director, then he has a job of staff organisation ahead of him before he begins to indulge in any PR campaign.

One of the aims of every library service should surely be to say 'yes' to users as much as possible. Rules are of course necessary for every organization, but it can hardly be denied that in the past many librarians and their staffs, to say nothing of their readers, have been hampered by unduly restrictive regulations. At the outset of a PR exercise therefore it might be a good thing for the librarian and his governing body to take a look at the rules of the library. By all means retain those regulations which are essential to the efficient running of the library, but ruthlessly eliminate those which are out-of-date and unnecessarily hampering.

It might be necessary too, to give some advice to personnel on the interpretation of the library's rules. People in many sectors of employment have demonstrated from time to time that by working to rule they can slow down operations to an almost unbearable point. The rules of some libraries are so many and complex that the staff, if they so minded, could apply them rigorously and by doing so almost cripple the service and certainly bring it into disrepute. To ensure that this state of affairs is never even approached, the wise governing body will give its director of libraries considerable discretion in the application of the rules, and the wise director should likewise give his responsible staff similar discretion.

We have all read from time to time of cases of high-handedness on the part of library staffs, and such overbearing attitudes almost always lead to bad public relations for the service. It is some comfort, though not much, to realize that public services generally are especially prone to this sort of thing. We know of bus conductors who unreasonably refuse to give change, and of drivers who turn blind eyes to passengers waiting at bus stops. Result – bad publicity; and all the considerate bus conductors and drivers who help to maintain regular and efficient services most of the time are forgotten against the minority of those of their colleagues, whose shortcomings are high-lighted. It can be the same in the library service. There was the reported story of the librarian who refused to admit to the library a handicapped person in an invalid chair because the rules of the library stated 'no wheeled vehicles admitted'. There is some doubt as to whether this incident really happened in the way in which it was reported, but if it did, then it was an instance of a reasonable rule being applied unreasonably.

When discretion is permitted mistakes will follow, but not nearly so many as will happen if the rules are rigidly applied. The lesson surely is that all library personnel should be trained and encouraged to apply regulations on the utilitarianist principle of the greatest good for the greatest number.

One other item of staff training affecting good public relations is in the use of telephone. There was a time when telephone manners generally left a lot to be desired, but some improvements have taken place thanks largely to campaigns undertaken by the telephone services themselves. Libraries especially cannot afford to relax in this matter. Personnel must be carefully trained to answer telephones promptly and clearly. The larger library services will, of course, have exchanges with trained telephone operators, but there are still many service-points, especially branch libraries, where library staff will be answering outside calls. The best practice is to announce the name of the library with the addition of the phrase 'can I help you?' This phrase should also be used by library staff on service desks when outside calls are being put through to them.

Management can help both staff and users by taking frequent checks of telephone traffic to ensure that the library has sufficient lines to cope with the demands made by telephone. It can be very frustrating when inquirers have to telephone the library several times, only to be greeted over and over again with the engaged signal. Another frustration for the telephone caller, particularly in these days of subscriber trunk dialling, is to be kept holding the line while waiting to be put through to an extension. Telephone operators should in such circumstances ask their callers to ring back, or else take the caller's number and ring him back when the required extension is free. It all contributes to satisfactory personal service, which is good PR in itself.

In correspondence too, the library should set the highest possible standards. These begin with the design of the headed notepaper and, judging from some of the examples seen, most chief librarians would do well to take a long, hard, objective look at their official notepaper. Sometimes librarians are shackled by the need to conform to the style of notepaper dictated by their parent bodies: this is a pity, but it need not signal the end of the librarian's influence since it has been known for librarians to have been instrumental in encouraging a re-design of their parent body's notepaper. Before changing letterheads, samples from the library display artist or from a good print designer should be studied, and the opportunity ought to be taken to co-ordinate the type on the headed notepaper with that used by the library for its annual reports, booklists, posters and even shelf guiding.

The contents and manner of correspondence can also be a vital factor in the library's good public relations. Every effort ought to be made to take the cold starchiness out of official letter-writing, and to replace it with a warmer person-to-person atmosphere.

This should begin with the salutation. I am not an admirer of the 'Dear Sir or Madam' approach, and in all but the most official letters we should write 'Dear Mr Hill' or 'Dear Mrs Jones' and end with 'Yours sincerely' rather than the colder 'Yours truly' or 'Yours faithfully'. While on this subject, may I suggest that we ought to use readers' names much more than we do when we are dealing with their inquiries on service desks? Most people, though admittedly not all, are pleased and flattered when hotel and airline receptionists address them by name, and it is noticeable that many banks have adopted this practice. A glance at the airline ticket, the credit card or the cheque enables this to be done, and in most libraries a glance at the user's ticket gives the opportunity to follow suit. A small thing this – but it can help to take something of the icy chill out of what may sometimes be regarded as a bureaucratic encounter by the library user.

In between the 'Dear Mr Hill' and the 'Yours sincerely' it is equally important to compose the letter in a warm and friendly style. To some letter-writers this comes naturally. To others it may be more difficult, but practice will help, and so may the perusal of a good book on the topic of letter-writing. When we are corresponding with our users, letters tend to fall into two or three main categories. We are either answering their inquiries and (we hope) giving them the information they seek, or else we are faced with the more unpleasant task of asking for the return of some overdue book or other material. In the latter instance it is especially necessary to be tactful and pleasant.

As we shall see from a later chapter I shall be recommending among other printed publicity a general folder outlining the services of the library, including a directory of addresses, telephone numbers, and hours of opening. It is a good idea to produce this in such a form that it will easily slip into a wallet or a pocket, and if it does this it will also slip into an envelope. Why not make a habit of slipping a copy into the envelope whenever we write to our users?

Printed postcards and pro-formae letters are awful stumbling blocks in the way of the librarian who is seeking to perfect his public relations. Obviously they are necessary and we must make use of them for reservations, for overdue notices, for informing users about the progress of their special requests, and for a number of other communications. My own experience, however, and that of many chief librarians, is that our users are extremely sensitive about the wording of such printed or duplicated communications. Cards informing users that reserved material is now ready for them at the library usually present no problem, for this is good news. It is in composing the texts of postcards and duplicated letters requesting the return of overdue material, or asking users to renew their tickets, or dunning them for overdue charges that the greatest care is needed.

It is little use saying to yourself that you are in the right and that it is the user who is in the wrong, even though this may be true most times. You must put yourself in the position of the recipient, and compose your text with diplomacy, making the pill as sweet as possible. Some time ago I had a few complaints about the text of a printed demand: not really many complaints but enough to make me look again at the text and make its less peremptory. Even after that, more complaints came in from sensitive people, so a further sweetening of the text took place. There have been no more complaints, To me, even one user lost to the library is a tragedy, and I am happy to think that we are no longer losing users on account of over-peremptory demands.

My final word of advice on this is to make frequent examinations of the number of printed and duplicated communications sent out by the library. Are they all really necessary? If not, ruthlessly cut out those that are being used so rarely that they can be replaced by a personal signed letter. With those that are left, carefully examine the text of all of them, and try to make them as clear and as friendly as possible. Edit the texts until you are satisfied that they say what has to be said, and that nobody could possibly take offence.

In all aspects of personal service from the library, gear yourself and your staff to adopt at all times a positive rather than a negative attitude. Create a library service that likes to say 'Yes' to its users, but on the occasions when you have to say 'No', then say it as nicely as possible.

Chapter 3
Librarians as print-users

Over the years librarians in most countries have been great users of print. Great quantitatively, but qualitatively? – not so impressive. We produce annual reports, library bulletins and magazines, printed catalogues, subject booklists, lists of recent additions, special service folders, book week programmes and the like, and great opportunities exist here to publicize libraries in attractive typographical styles. Here and there the opportunies have been taken, but it has to be remarked with regret that the good examples are few, standing out like beacons in an otherwise undistinguished mass.

In the foreword to William R. Holman's beautiful book *Library publications,* Lawrence Clark Powell comments that 'Library printing throughout California and most of the United States has been undistinguished'. Dr Powell was kind enough, or tactful enough, not to mention other countries where, on the whole, the general level is even more undistinguished than the examples he complains about in his own country. In commending Holman's book, which all practising and student librarians should surely peruse, he does offer some hope for future improvements. 'Library education', he writes, 'is recognizing a need for training in . . . elements of taste and learning', and he goes on to say: 'A neophyte librarian whose education has included such experience will not gladly accept shoddy printing in the library where he goes to work'.

Holman's book is a work of art in itself, a splendid example endowed with much practical advice and inspiring instances of actual print produced by some of the best American libraries. Holman himself has no doubt about the important effects of good typography and design. 'It is imperative', he says, 'that the library evoke and stimulate interest in its resources, services and objectives through the appeal of tasteful design. A

30

piece of printing invariably reflects the philosophy and tone of the source producing it. Make yours speak in such a warm, lively and colourful style that even the most jaded patron will feel a new awareness of the library's importance'.

It is only fair to assert that there have been movements in the past directed towards improving the typographical image of libraries. In the 1930s a group of young librarians concerned with the monthly journal of the Association of Assistant Librarians campaigned widely and with some influence on behalf of good library printing. Stanley Snaith and others regularly reviewed library publications in Britain, lambasted the shoddy ones, and were encouraging in their praise towards any showing a spark of originality and taste. But such campaigns flare up, have a limited influence for good, and then they die down and we are back to the bad old ways.

It has been said that good printing is no more expensive than shoddy printing, but this is not entirely true, especially in provincial towns where jobbing printers have limited ranges of founts available. There seem to be two main reasons why library printing is so often drab and uninspired. One is lack of money. Library budgets are often so tight that librarians feel themselves lucky to have just enough money to indulge in print for publicity purposes, and they then readily accept poor typography and design in order to produce print at all. But not all the blame can be laid at the door of financial stringency. Lack of taste and feeling is also present in the profession, and some librarians with reasonable budgets still produce bad print because they either know no better, or they just do not care.

Fortunately, as in the United States, library schools in the United Kingdom and other countries are concerning themselves increasingly with improving knowledge and taste in the field of typography and print design. As Lawrence Clark Powell observed, there are signs that the newer products of library education have higher standards and will seek to indulge them when they have the opportunities to do so.

Much has been done, and can be done, to raise standards through the encouragement of good example. For a number of years the John Cotton Dana Awards scheme has had an increasingly good effect upon the originality, attractiveness and appearance of library publications. And not just in the United States, for a number of libraries outside America, Islington for one, has received awards and citations from that source. In the United Kingdom a similar scheme was started by the journal *The Library World* in the 1960s and ran for several successful years before a change of ownership caused a gap, temporary one hopes. While *The Library World* Publicity Awards scheme was active there was increasing evidence that both British and overseas librarians were interested in it, and that more were thinking positively about the appearance of their printed publicity.

ANNUAL REPORTS

Not all libraries issue annual reports but many do so, and for some it is their major printing activity. When this is the case, and indeed at all times, the annual report should be regarded as a major PR document. All the more reason why the utmost care should be lavished on its physical appearance and presentation.

Because the annual report sets out to be an accurate and historical record of work done, supported by statistics, there is a tendency for it to be written in formal prose tailored for committee consumption. Occasionally a librarian has departed from tradition, as did J. D. Stewart at Bermondsey years ago when he wrote his annual report in a chatty, informal style, but this has rarely been repeated by his colleagues. Nevertheless, in the writing of the report, the advantages of short paragraphs and catchy headings should not be lost sight of. Given then that the annual report has these traditional shackles, it is all the more important that when it is printed it should be presented as attractively as possible, otherwise it may not be read.

The cover design is all important. If the library staff includes a professional display artist he should be given the opportunity of producing designs for this. If not, it would be money well spent to utilise the services of an outside typographical artist who might also be responsible for choosing the type faces and designing the interior layout. The layout should, if possible, include illustrations and perhaps a diagrammatic map showing library locations. If the librarian is to have a good choice of illustrations he should be on the *qui vive* for possibilities throughout the year. Colourful displays in the libraries should be photographed for possible use in the annual report, while other illustrations might include views of new library buildings, children's activities in the libraries, housebound services in action, exhibition openings, book week activities, close-ups of rare books and manuscripts acquired, and before-and-after photographs of modernization schemes. The subjective approach must be constantly borne in mind: in other words, photographs should include people when possible, and it is always better if the pictures are not obviously posed.

What about the presentation of statistics? These are rightly given in a standardized form as an aid to comparison, but there is no reason why they should not be given added prominence by including among them graphs and charts. Here again a good artist is essential.

The general interior layout should avoid blank spaces and blank pages. The back and inside covers can be used to print names of committee members and a list of senior staff, or else the diagrammatic map previously mentioned.

If formality must prevail due to local requirements, there are several ways in which the impact can be softened. One is by issuing an attractive folder with the annual report in which the report's main points are emphasized. Another is by using the middle-page spread of the printed report to highlight its principal paragraphs and figures. Yet another is to issue a press release with the report. All these will encourage and help journalists to mention the publication, but without them a formal document is at a grave disadvantage on an editor's desk.

Much can be learnt from studying good examples of annual reports, outside the library field as well as in it. Toronto Public Libraries have maintained a very high standard over the years, and there are other exemplary products from overseas, including Western Australia, Canberra, Tanzania, Denver, Stockholm and elsewhere. In Britain, Camden, Lambeth, Lincoln, Luton, Southwark and Westminster have won

B

awards. The new and larger public library authorities which will begin fresh eras of progress in England and Wales in 1974 would do well to consider starting new series of annual reports, concentrating particularly upon their design and presentation.

PRINTED CATALOGUES AND LIBRARY BULLETINS

Another publishing activity of many libraries is the production of printed catalogues. I refer not so much to general catalogues as to those covering special collections, either of the locality, or of individual authors or of special subjects. Most libraries have special collections of which they are proud, and it would seem an obvious activity sooner or later to produce catalogues of these in permanent form. Such catalogues can be put on sale to the public and other libraries. Because of this, the librarian must assess as carefully as he can the size of the edition, at the same time ensuring that this permanent record is accurate, well-indexed, and well designed and printed. Attractively produced, such catalogues can be an additional element in the library's PR programme, and more libraries should be producing them for their bibliographical value as well as their promotional possibilities.

The library bulletin, appearing in the form of a monthly or quarterly magazine, is not so common now as it was before 1939, but examples still exist, notably at Camden, Swindon and elsewhere. The object of such publications was to list and annotate recent additions to the library, to include feature articles on the work of authors or about books on various subjects, and to add paragraphs about library news such as staff changes, new library projects, changes in opening hours and the like. Printing costs can be lessened by the introduction of advertisements, which some librarians deplore in library publications, but which can surely be justified if they are appropriate to books and reading. A small charge may also be made to readers purchasing the bulletin, though it might be decided to issue the publication free to readers.

BOOKLISTS

Those libraries which do not aspire to the production of periodical bulletins will still find it necessary to issue lists of recent additions in some form or other, and special subject lists from time to time. The popular format for recent additions lists is the folder, the size of which usually limits the contents to authors and titles, prohibiting annotations. Even so, they can be made attractive by careful design, by the use of a recognizable library symbol, by using catchy headings, and by employing different colours for each issue. This latter is important, for if the list is always printed in the same colour, readers do not quickly appreciate that a new one is available.

If the library cannot afford even to produce additions lists in cheap folder form, there are other ways of getting this information over to users. One is to supply lists to the local press, since many editors are pleased to feature these on a regular basis. Another is to make use of the PR bulletin which an increasing number of local authorities are producing centrally through their own PROs. When this is the case, the librarian should try to ensure that the library is allotted a regular column for listing additions to stock, and also that it gets a feature article occasionally.

Every library's print programme should include regular publication of special booklists, either devoted to specific subjects or to individual authors of groups of authors. Topicality should be the keynote, and a watchful eye should be kept on forthcoming anniversaries and on the press for subjects in the news. Local circumstances should also be borne in mind, such as the possibility of printing a key list of reference books in a highly developed business and commercial area, a list of books on hotel-keeping and catering for a seaside community, or a list of books on farming and the countryside to be put on a library exhibition stand at an agricultural fair.

Radio and TV forthcoming programmes should be studied, for experience has shown that these often lead to an increase in reading books related to them. Archaeology, antiques, astronomy, gardening, chess, economics, music and the fine arts

35

have all provided past examples of reading revivals caused by TV. Nor is the interest confined to subjects. Historical personages such as Henry VIII, Elizabeth I and others have been featured on TV and stimulated demands for books about them and their periods, while series and serials by classic authors such as Jane Austen, Mrs Gaskell, Dickens, Thackeray, Alcott, Zola and Galsworthy have the same effect. The librarian who forecasts these interests and demands, taking the opportunity to prepare and publish timely booklists about them, is wise and truly PR conscious.

Attractive, printed folder form is often acceptable for these special booklists, but if the budget permits, the more major booklists should be prepared in booklet form. Many topics lend themselves to this longer treatment – such subjects as Africa, the Common Market, the Charles Dickens' centenary among them.

The subject list in booklet form lends itself to more exhaustive and ambitious treatment than the folder type. A compelling cover is essential, an introduction or foreword is desirable, and readable annotations should be added to many if not all the entries. Quotations at the head of each section might be considered, and typographical decorations can be introduced to good advantage. The full catalogue type of entry should be avoided like the plague, and strict cataloguing rules can be ignored with impunity. Authors' names should be reproduced in their best-known form and, in any printed list, forenames and initials should precede surnames. Examples of other libraries' subject lists should be critically studied, not forgetting that probably more can be learned from the bad specimens than from the good.

SERVICE LEAFLETS

Every library should have constantly in print a general leaflet or folder outlining the scope of its services, and including a directory of library addresses and telephone numbers as well as opening hours. A diagrammatic map showing locations might also be included. The main aim of such a leaflet is to present it to new users, but it could also be in any circulars which are despatched from the library. Since it is somewhat in the nature of a throwaway leaflet and will be produced in quantity there is a case for having it printed on thin paper, but there is still no excuse for bad design or typography. In fact it should be as arresting as possible in its physical appearance. Long paragraphs of prose should be avoided: its points should be made in short jabs so that people will be encouraged to read and remember it. The size of such a general leaflet or folder is important, and consideration should be given to producing it in such a size that it will easily fit into a wallet or an envelope.

Another form of printed library publicity are leaflets or folders on various special services. These will be mentioned more fully in a later chapter, but the sort of things I have in mind are leaflets devoted to children's services, adult lending services, reference and information aspects, music and record libraries, mobile library services, deliveries to the housebound, or any other special services or collections the library wishes to publicize. Some libraries issue such folders with a standardized front cover, altering only the title and having a different colour for each one: others prefer to have individual cover designs for every one, and this is probably better.

In this jet age libraries everywhere are experiencing more visitors and users from countries other than their own, and it is interesting to note that many metropolitan libraries have had the initiative to produce basic information on their services in foreign languages. This is becoming increasingly necessary in Europe. A number of Scandinavian libraries led the way, and the Stockholm Public Library has produced a short introduction for foreign visitors in English. Malmö and Gothenburg have done likewise, and there are other examples from Holland, Germany, Hungary and the USSR. The All-Union State Library for Foreign Literature in Moscow has issued a well-designed and illustrated guide not only in English but in other foreign languages as well.

Few British libraries have done much in this direction, but the day is surely coming when it will have to be considered. Not only are more foreign visitors coming to our libraries, there is the problem of newly-arrived immigrants as well, some of whom arrive in the United Kingdom with little or no know-ledge of the English language. It is a nice gesture to be able to present foreign visitors, not only with the library's PR material in English, but also with an outline in French or German or another foreign language. And if we wish, as we surely should, immigrants to come to our libraries and use them, we might at least have brief introductions in languages they understand, whether it be Greek or Spanish, Urdu or Gujurati.

It is not suggested, in the first place, that these should be printed. A duplicated or multilithed version would be wel-comed, although later experience may persuade the librarian to introduce printed versions, as Stockholm did with its intro-duction in English.

DUPLICATED AND IMITATION TYPESCRIPT PRODUCTIONS

Mention of the duplicator reminds us that we are not confined to traditional printing for all our publicity. Librarians operat-ing on shoestring budgets, and this includes all of us from time to time, have made great use of the duplicator and the multi-lith. Computer typesetting has offered a new alternative in recent years.

Nevertheless, departures from traditional print should never be made unless economy dictates them, or except where specialized publicity requires only very short runs which will not justify the use of print. If imitation typescript or duplicated methods have to be used, the utmost care should be taken in design and presentation. A combination of print and imitation typescript is often possible, having the front cover printed for maximum attractiveness. Furthermore, modern methods of reproduction are very sophisticated, permitting the use of illus-trations and drawings to lighten the effect. Different coloured papers may be put to good use. With a merging of all these elements – printed cover, introduction of drawings and decor-ations, the use of colour, added to an accurate and lively con-tent – a well-produced addition may be added to the library's PR material.

Some excellent examples of duplicated, multilithed or computer set publicity may be seen, and these should be studied
carefully. Holman's book previously mentioned contains a
number of good specimens from American public and college
libraries, and it is perhaps a consolation to librarians elsewhere
to see that large libraries such as those of San Francisco,
Detroit and Philadelphia often find it necessary to augment
their more ambitious print programmes with items produced
more cheaply. There are increasingly good instances of this
type of work from British and European libraries too, but alas!
still too many poor specimens rear their ugly heads. As with
good and bad print. I sometimes think more can be learned
from a perusal of the tatty and careless productions than from
the better ones. Before embarking on a duplicated or imitation
typescript production, the librarian should ask himself what is
the object and who comprise the audience. He should also
remember that however small the audience the finished production will remain an advertisement, good or bad, for his
library. It must then be his aim to use every device and all
possible expertise and imagination to ensure that it will be a
good advertisement.

OUTLETS FOR PRINTED PUBLICITY

When the finished product, printed or duplicated, arrives on
his desk, there is sometimes a tendency for the librarian to wash
his hands of the project and perhaps to start thinking of his
next venture into print on behalf of the library. Too little
thought is often given to the distribution of PR materials, much
of which have been produced as a result of a good deal of work
and forethought. It is just not good enough to distribute them
to library service desks, leaving users to pick them up at their
whim.

How then to consider more effective ways of distributing the
library's publicity materials?

The wise librarian will not start to think about this when the
finished products arrive, he will in fact have considered it much
earlier, perhaps even when the concept was first planned. It

39

has already been said that size is important, and that publicity leaflets and folders should be made to fit into envelopes of preferred size. This is because mailing can be one of the main outlets for library publicity. The throwaway general service leaflet or folder can often be mailed, either slipped in with normal correspondence or, if a new library is due to be opened and a letter is being sent to local residents, it can be included with that.

Special beaming of PR by mail must never be lost sight of. There may be occasions when school teachers should be sent a certain book list or folder; business men should be circulated with any material referring to the commercial or reference library; art schools and their students should receive appropriate booklists on art or material on the collection of art books; a religious booklist should be sent to churches and ministers; music academies and schools should be on the mailing list for recent additions to the music and gramophone record libraries; and so on, *ad infinitum*.

It is vital that the library's own mailing-list is kept up-to-date and that care is taken to use the latest editions of directories and reference books if these are being utilized for mailing purposes. People are rightly touchy if they are incorrectly addressed and a lot of the care taken in planning and producing library PR material can go awry if this happens.

One final point. Libraries which produce many publicity specimens should also use an attractively designed wallet in which their material can be included *en masse*. This is just another sign of efficiency and forethought which can do the library nothing but good.

Chapter 4
Relations with press, radio, TV and other media

It has to be admitted that libraries have not had a very good image of themselves projected through the media of the press, radio, TV and films. The aspects of library service which have been publicized have been precisely those which most librarians would prefer to be forgotten. The inevitable elements of a library cartoon in a newspaper or magazine concentrate upon the repressive, such as commanding 'Silence' notices, or upon the archaic, such as library interiors with shelving from floor to ceiling, while librarians themselves are always portrayed as shabby, decrepit, myopic, absent-minded creatures. New stories too tend to concentrate on the bureaucratic attitudes of librarians, and little or no interest is shown in the progressive, imaginative and valuable services rendered by the profession to the community.

Librarians are not alone in suffering such treatment, for many other professions make the same complaint. It seems to be the way of the world that editors are interested only in bad news which can be played up in a sensational manner: good news is unexciting, therefore to be ignored. I am not criticizing editors, merely stating a fact: editors, like librarians, are the servants of the public, and since they have to sell their products to the public they give the public what it wants.

Another factor militates against libraries in their quest for publicity, and this is that editors and journalists are much more interested in subjective news than in the objective. This means people as against things. A story about a mother who is made to keep her baby in a perambulator outside the library in inclement weather by a callous and unthinking librarian is worth half-a-column as an example of bureaucratic repression, while a report of the library which has made outstanding progress in the last year will rate much less space, because people and personalities are not involved. Again, one is not being critical of the press: it is the way of the journalistic world. People, not things, make the most readable news, and readable news is what editors must give their readers.

One reason why libraries have traditionally had such a bad press is that librarians have failed to appreciate these elementary facts of PR life. They have also not realized the importance of presenting the library pictorially through good photographs, charts or graphs. It is no good sending editors a dull, routine report of library progress, unenlivened with subject interest, unsupported by pictorial matter, and expecting the press to give it prominence. Too much of this sort of thing has happened in the past, which is just one reason why the old image of libraries persists.

Some librarians have already appreciated the importance of living with contemporary PR needs. They have learnt their lessons, with the result that they have gained increasingly good publicity for their libraries. But despite these achievements, and despite a discernible improvement in the PR image of libraries and librarians, many more need to acquire an awareness of what the mass media, and their editors, are looking for in the way of news stories, press releases and illustrative material about libraries.

PRESS RELEASES

The press release is a mid-twentieth-century phenomenon and is now used extensively by all kinds of organizations. The result is that editors' desks are flooded with such papers. Editors are only human, so it is natural that they will notice those press releases which are brief, informative, attractive and conform to their requirements. Librarians, for their part, are inspiring more and more press releases, either prepared by themselves or else by their PROs on their behalf. It may be assumed that a trained PRO knows all about the art of writing good press releases, so the following remarks are really directed to those librarians intending to prepare the releases themselves.

Attractiveness is of prime importance. Those larger libraries which intend to issue numerous press releases should have specially designed and headed duplicating paper, so that the sheet is readily identifiable. A precise subject heading should be given, but there need be no attempt to write a press headline, that is the job of a sub-editor. Ideally, the typing should be double-spaced as usual with press submissions, with a good margin on the left.

Brevity is the next essential. There is a natural tendency on the part of all news release writers to try to pack in the maximum information on the grounds that the more that is written the more will be printed. Nothing could be further from the truth. In fact the press release should understate rather than overstate the case: it should titivate the editor's interest by perhaps even deliberately omitting some salient points. This may very well encourage him to initiate a telephone call for more information. So be informative by all means, but also be brief, and do not forget to include the phrase 'For further information please contact Mr . . .' together with the telephone number and extension. Needless to say, the person to be contacted in the library should be the one who has the answers to all possible questions.

It is sometimes necessary to place an embargo on the date and hour of release of the news. Editors appreciate this information. Midnight is a favourite hour, since TV and radio may have closed down by then, and this gives newspaper editors the opportunity to include the news in the next morning's paper without being scooped by his broadcasting colleagues. It is rarely that library publicity falls within this urgent category but the point is worth mentioning.

What sort of library news merits a press release? More perhaps than may be realized. The opening of a new library building, the inauguration of a new service, the visit of an eminent personage or an international group to the library, the arrival of a foreign librarian as part of a staff exchange, the inauguration of a book week, the opening of an exhibition, the start of a series of lectures or recitals, the selection of a member of the professional staff for a consultancy overseas – these are just a few examples. Do not forget to include a photograph if possible, or alternatively invite the editor to send a photographer to the library in connection with the press release.

Finally, there is the question of to whom shall the release be sent? An impressive amount of time, money, stationery and postage can be wasted by a blanket despatch of press releases, and it is better to be selective. The local press and professional journals might normally be sent everything, but national newspapers and magazines should be carefully chosen for inclusion in the mailing list. It is the same with radio and TV. Press releases will normally always be sent to editors of news programmes on local radio stations, but only exceptionally will they be issued to the national networks.

PRESS CONFERENCES

The press conference, as opposed to the press release, is something that librarians will convene only occasionally. The most common occasion for a press conference is in connection with the impending opening of an important new library building, and this event, like all press conferences needs careful pre-planning. The arrangements may not be in the librarian's hands at all, for in the case of a major new building, the architects or the governing body of the library may employ professional PR consultants to organize the press conference. Even so, the librarian will still be closely involved, and if the new building is a small or medium-sized library, he may have complete control over the arrangements.

Press conferences in connection with new buildings are normally arranged before the official opening ceremony, sometimes several days before. The object of this private view is to give journalists the opportunity, which they will welcome, of seeing the whole building in company with the various experts who have been concerned with its planning and erection – the architect, the quantity surveyor, the builder and the librarian. Talks to assembled journalists at a press conference should be kept brief, but the opportunities for questions should be unlimited.

Before the press conference the architect and the librarian

will have co-operated in the production of handout material containing facts and figures about the new library. Photographs, both exterior and interior, should be supplied in profusion, and these will almost certainly have been taken by professional photographers who will have sought the advice of both architect and librarian as to the features to be concentrated upon. Panoramic interior views of the various departments should be supported by detailed pictures of shelving, furniture and equipment. The whole of the handout material, including photographs and brochures, should be issued to the visiting journalists in a handy press kit.

It is customary to serve cocktails or wine with buffet refreshments at press conferences. It should not be thought for one moment that this will necessarily attract any more journalists than would otherwise have come, for in fact the press receives so many invitations of this kind that it is just part of the day's work! Nevertheless, many hard-working journalists may have travelled some distance to attend the press conference and will appreciate some refreshment as they listen to the talk, study the handout material, and tour the library. In any case, the library cannot afford to be compared badly with other organizations who arrange press conferences.

The really important point about press conferences is that the invitations should be sent out well in advance of the time. Like everybody else these days, editors work to a calendar and their diaries, and those of their staff, get increasingly full. Not only is it unfair to spring press conferences upon editors at short notice, it will result in a disappointing turnout of journalists. The same, by the way, applies to press releases, which should also be circulated well in advance.

Finally, the press conference should be organized as meticulously as an official opening itself. Consider the timing well in advance, work to an agenda, and try to ensure that speakers, whether architects or librarians, do not overstep their time allotments.

NEWSPAPER STORIES AND MAGAZINE ARTICLES

Some librarians, working on their own and without the help of a professional PRO, prefer to send out newspaper stories from time to time to selected editors. Much good publicity can result from this activity, but care is needed in handling this technique. Those librarians, and there are many, who are experienced writers, can often produce a telling story which an editor may print in its entirety. But not all librarians are capable of this, and some advice may be necessary.

No story of this kind is likely to be printed in a newspaper unless it has subjective interest, in other words it must be about people, or a particular person. If the story concerns a member of the library staff, the use of a name may be desirable, but if it is about a user of the library it may be necessary not to include the name. If in doubt, submit a draft to the person concerned to see if he has any objection to his name being mentioned in the story.

The next requirement is to write as closely as possible to the idiom of the paper to which the story is being submitted. The style used in *The Guardian* is different from that used in the *Daily Mirror*, and both are different from that which may be used in a local newspaper. Careful study of the newspaper's general style should be made before submitting a story. Remember to write the story without frills: keep it brief and keep it crisp. Remember too that a newspaper story is not a press release: select the newspaper of your choice and submit your story to that paper and that alone. If an editor suspects that a story had been submitted to other papers at the same time as his own, the submission is doomed for a quick end in the wastepaper basket.

Magazine articles are an entirely different proposition, and perhaps librarians have never given enough thought to this form of publicity. During the 1967 National Library Week in Britain a determined and deliberate attempt was successfully made to publicize libraries through the medium of articles in journals and magazines, but this was corporate publicity for the service in general rather than advertising a particular library and its wares. Nevertheless, individual librarians could give more thought to publicizing their libraries via locally published journals. Reference to the *Writers' and Artists' Year Book* may yield a number of outlets for the British librarian, and there are, of course, similar reference books in other countries. County and regional magazines are possible outlets, while in metropolitan city areas there are usually a large number of journals published whose editors might be interested in a well-written, illustrated article on the library service in general. If the library possesses any special collections consideration should be given towards beaming articles on these to specialist journals.

In preparing magazine articles the same care and attention should be given as with newspaper stories: study the character and style of each journal and present the article in the required length, with or without illustrations according to the needs of the magazine. A preliminary letter to the editor is sometimes a good idea: if his reply is discouraging then no further time need be wasted. The importance of photographs must not be overlooked, for a majority of magazines like to include them with articles. For this and other purposes the librarian should keep a dossier of up-to-date photographs of library buildings, their interiors, and of the various services in action. Photographs of library activities should include people, and they are always more effective if they have been taken spontaneously without obvious posing.

The cultivation of good relations with editors, particularly those in the locality, will undoubtedly lead to an encouraging flow of publicity for the library. It may also cause editors and journalists to get into the habit of telephoning the librarian for further information say, on a committee minute, and sometimes the press will get into the habit of telephoning on the off-chance of finding out if there is any interesting news of library affairs. If editors once get the idea that librarians are publicity conscious, they will go out of their way to encourage this. Telephone calls of this kind can sometimes be embarrassing, and the librarian may sometimes feel that he is not at liberty to divulge some development which is perhaps not finalized. Nevertheless, he should say as much as he can, and be as frank as possible. It is my experience that editors and journalists respect confidences, and are themselves anxious to give libraries as good a press as they can.

Because the press is interested in the subjective approach, the librarian who cultivates good relations with editors may inevitably find that his own name and photograph appear with a rather dangerous regularity. I use the word dangerous because most librarians are public officials and the cult of the personality is sometimes resented by governing bodies and by the public at large. The wise librarian will be on the lookout for over-exposure of his own name. One way to avoid this is to issue news stories and press releases with mention, not of the librarian's own name but of first one, then another, senior librarian who happens to be concerned with the developments being publicized. This is good staff relations as well as good public relations. A first-class library service is the result of team-work and he is a poor chief librarian who tries to claim the credit for everything. Another way in which the personality cult can be checked is by having a private word with the editor concerned, asking him to make fewer references to your name in his references to the library. Most editors will see the point and will co-operate.

LIAISON WITH PUBLIC RELATIONS OFFICERS

Library services, whether university, government or public, are not only themselves increasing in size and import, they are becoming part of larger organizations. More such organizations are directly employing public relations officers, and when this is the case it is vital for the librarian to collaborate closely with the PRO. Conversations should be held at an early stage to clear some important points. Does the PRO intend to produce a regular bulletin or journal, and if so, how can the library contribute to this? By news stories, by feature articles, by annotated select lists of recent additions? Does the PRO want the librarian to channel all library publicity through him? Would he object to the librarian dealing directly with local and other

make time to read

---

ask at your local Westminster public library for leaflets covering the Diary of Events, Children's Activities and National and Local Competitions to be held during

NATIONAL LIBRARY WEEK
12-19 MARCH 1966

WESTMINSTER LOCAL COMMITTEE FOR NATIONAL LIBRARY WEEK

A poster in royal blue for Britain's first National Library Week incorporates the NLW symbol and a diagrammatic representation of Westminster's coat-of-arms.

You've got a right to read. Don't blow it.

NATIONAL
LIBRARY WEEK
PROGRAM
1971

National
Library
Week

a

festival

of

books

8-15 March 1969

Two NLW bookmarks. *Left :* An American example of 1971 and (*right*) a more sober design from Britain in 1969. But the British bookmark was printed in white on red, and the American, more sombre, was printed in white on black.

ANY NUMBER OF TEACHERS
CAN PLAY

THE LIBRARY GAME

NOW YOU CAN BE A WINNER!

**ENOCH PRATT
FREE LIBRARY**

Baltimore's Enoch Pratt Free Library cashes in on people's interest in dice games. Inside the four-page leaflet opens up on sixteen squares à la Monopoly. Square 15 asserts 'There is no MONOPOLY on joy in reading'.

The Clements Library at the University of Michigan, Ann Arbor is a collection of early American history, housed with dignity. The front cover of its twelve-sided folder reflects this dignity, while inside are photographs and information about it manuscript division and other services.

editors? Does the PRO employ an official photographer, and if so, is it obligatory for the librarian to use his services? These and other questions are basic, and if the librarian and the PRO are to work profitably together, they should be discussed and settled at the outset. The wise librarian will supply his PRO with all possible information about his service so that the PRO begins with a sound background knowledge of the resources and objectives of the library. With this at his disposal he will be able to put library news into its proper perspective, and may suggest to the librarian areas of potential publicity. Since the PRO will probably be an experienced journalist, he will always be looking out for news of subjective interest. Staff promotions and examination successes, staff exchanges, the arrival of a foreign intern librarian, the occasion of an international visit, the work of children's librarians and those concerned with the housebound service – all these and more are grist to the mill of the PRO.

The good PRO will not absolutely insist on all library publicity being channelled through his office, for he will realize that the librarian, like all heads of departments, receives telephone calls from the press, and that it would be bureaucracy gone mad if he had to refer these to the PRO, who in turn would have to telephone the librarian for the answers. On the other hand the PRO will rightly insist on having the fullest advance notice of major developments, and of handling the publicity for these. A good working arrangement is for the librarian to be allowed to send minor news stories to the press, but of course to send copies to the PRO for his information.

There is a great need to keep the PRO and his staff fully educated and up-to-date on the library service. If the librarian holds, as he should, meetings of his senior staff, it is a good idea to invite the PRO or his representative to sit in from time to time. By merely listening, the PRO will often pick up information which he can usefully publicize, information which the librarian and his staff might never have conceived as potential PR material.

RADIO AND TV PROGRAMMES

Opportunities for librarians to appear on radio and TV are limited, but they should be eagerly seized when they come along. In small built-up countries like Britain where national TV and radio programmes have been much more prominent than local ones it has been particularly difficult for librarians to break into these media, but the situation has recently changed with the advent of many local radio stations. Now, as has happened in the United States for many years, librarians are getting more frequent opportunities to give radio talks on aspects of library service.

Conferences offer good chances of getting libraries in the round on TV and radio. When in a foreign country I am always impressed with the PR consciousness of foreign colleagues when, as in Hungary, they filmed part of the opening session of the 1972 IFLA Council for television or, as in Finland, they arrange for visiting foreign librarians to be interviewed for radio. All organizers of library conferences, at whatever level, should make every effort to interest TV and radio editors in their proceedings.

But how can the individual librarian obtain publicity for his library through TV or radio? There are numerous possibilities the best chance coming perhaps through the librarian's own PRO, if he is working with one in the same organization. The PRO has contacts which most librarians cannot hope to have, and it has often happened that a routine piece of library news passed on by the librarian to his PRO has resulted in a radio talk or interview.

If the librarian is not working through a PRO, and is issuing his own press releases, he should remember to send these to the news editors of TV and radio, and not just confine his circularization to press editors. Such press releases may be ignored, but they do frequently lead to mentions in news bulletins, or even requests for the librarian to give a short talk or to be interviewed.

Opportunities need not end here. The librarian, like a free-lance writer, may decide to submit a script for a radio talk.

If he does, he should study the market as carefully as he would study a newspaper or magazine to which he submits a story or an article. Radio programmes should be scrutinized for their content: it might be futile to submit a talk on commercial and business library facilities to a radio programme designed for women's listening, but the editor of the same programme could well be interested in a talk on library work with young children, or one on delivering books to housebound people.

Unsolicited material needs careful preparation. The length of talks on the programme should be studied, and your submission should be tailored to this length. Sentences should be short and uninvolved and, for general listening, the vocabulary used should be straightforward and comprehensible. It should not be an essay: instead, examples should be used, and subjective interest should be introduced whenever possible.

If an unsolicited talk is accepted, the librarian will be asked to visit the studio with his script either for a recording or a live broadcast. The producer will give him a brief coaching, sometimes all too brief, and before he knows where he is, the librarian will be on the air. If it is a recording there is not too much to worry about, for if the speaker loses his voice, gets lost in his script, or goes on too long, the producer will arrange a re-run. It is obviously not a good thing to try the patience of the producer too much, for even when recording he is working to a time schedule.

If the radio talk is to be given live, it is rather a different matter. When the red light goes on you are on the air and there is no turning back. The speaker will of course have rehearsed his script several times, and there should be no occasion for him to stumble or to exceed his time. The general tendency these days is for talks to be recorded, and for only interviews to go out live, but you cannot always rely on this. Whenever a speaker is broadcasting live I always hope, for his sake, that he has already made some recorded broadcasts and has so got over his microphone fright. Some people profess never to have had microphone fright: that may be so, but such speakers must be in a small minority. Faced with a live broadcast on one's very first visit to a studio can be a petrifying experience. It is much better if one can get experience through recordings

51

before being asked to do a live broadcast. It must be said however, that for most people microphone fright does not last long, and once you are over it you are through with it for ever.

Broadcasters need not worry about their accents. These are almost welcomed nowadays. If you speak naturally, at normal speed and without affectation, you will come over well. But any attempt to assume an accent which is not your own will be magnified by the microphone, and the result could be disastrous.

Interviews are much more common than straight talks, and they are easier to cope with. Again there may be very little coaching or rehearsal, but the interviewer may give one or two hints beforehand about the questions he is going to ask. Answers, by the way, should not be too long: if they are, there will soon be frantic signs from the producer behind his glass panel.

So much for radio, but what about TV, that other medium which, being visual, does not offer so many opportunities for library publicity? It is true that TV films about libraries are few and far between, but librarians' appearances in news and magazine programmes are gradually increasing. Such appearances will almost always be in the form of interviews, sometimes recorded, sometimes live. Much the same rules apply as for radio. Keep answers brief, though not monosyllabic: the subject who replies yes or no to every question is the despair of the interviewer. Ignore the camera, indeed never look at it unless you are giving a brief talk and are told to look towards the lens.

A first TV appearance can be daunting. It is not like radio where you just sit before the microphone and get on with it. With TV there are so many preliminaries – lighting arrangements, sound tests, make-up – all these and more have to be endured patiently, so there is a natural tendency to build up some nervous tension. Again it will help if it is a telerecording and not a live performance.

Experience of a TV studio is a help, but few librarians can acquire much experience of this kind. Fortunately, a number of organizations now realize the need to coach their executives who may from time to time be exposed on TV. Large businesses have pointed the way in this respect, but some large local authorities have followed suit, and Cheshire County Council is one example of a local authority which arranged for its senior executives to have coaching and practice in TV appearances. This trend is likely to increase in future.

Whether he is appearing on radio or TV, the librarian would do well to practise with a tape-recorder. A radio talk especially can be rehearsed this way, but in any case the tape-recorder is a useful instrument of self-criticism, and practice with it can do much to improve one's delivery.

I propose to say very little about films. A number of documentary films have been made about libraries, none of them very good. There is in fact a crying need for an outstanding library film. But when this is made, as it surely will be in the future, it will be made by professional film-makers and with a professional cast. A librarian may write the original script, and a librarian will surely give technical advice, but that will be the limit of our contribution to it as a profession.

Chapter 5
Co-operative library publicity

All libraries are basically doing the same thing, that is, supplying books and information to users, though they all may do it differently. Some are general in character, some are special, and they are providing their services for different groups of people. Nevertheless, there is enough uniformity in library services to allow for a co-operative approach in the matter of publicity. There is a tendency for the librarian of today to imagine that co-operative library publicity is a recent development, but there is nothing new under the sun, and librarians of previous generations thought in this way and many have acted together.

There are many obvious economies if libraries act co-operatively. Booklists, reading lists and posters are just three PR materials which can be produced much more cheaply in bulk for use by many libraries than if they are produced individually with much shorter print runs. Book weeks can be organized quite successfully by individual libraries, but their impact can be even greater if they form part of a regional or national effort. In this chapter we shall be looking at the influence of library associations on co-operative library publicity, and also trying to make some evaluation of the effect of National Library Weeks.

PR AND LIBRARY ASSOCIATIONS

Modern advertising methods, as we know them today, began in the United States and although other countries are rapidly catching up, it is to America that we still look for new ideas in advertising, and for the liveliest interest in public relations. The American Library Association has, not unnaturally, always been active in co-operative PR, and it has led library associations in other countries to follow suit. In Scandinavia, in West Germany and other countries, library associations have played important roles in establishing library supply agencies. These often began as co-operative ventures for library binding, but soon entered the fields of co-operative cataloguing, the supply of standardized stationery, furniture, equipment and library accessories and, most important of all from our point of view, they began to produce co-operative booklists, reading lists, bookmarks, posters and other printed material which could be bought by individual libraries for their own use or for passing on to readers either free or at an extremely low nominal cost.

Some examples of these might be quoted. In Sweden the Bibliotekstjänst, or Library Service Ltd., which started in 1951 but can trace its origins back to 1936, has produced a great variety of co-operative publicity. Most important of these have been their co-operative guides and booklists, mainly for use by librarians as book selection tools, but also useful to purposeful readers. More specifically for readers has been BTJ's publication *Wanderings with books*, comprising guides to subject literature with the general reader in mind. Many other periodical booklists and reading guides both for adults and children have been produced for libraries by BTJ, which has also initiated many pamphlets, folders and posters designed to attract and introduce readers to libraries.

The Norwegian Biblioteksentralen (Library Central Ltd.) has since 1958 had a bibliographical department with a specialized staff producing many standard booklists, indexes and other publications with a PR value. Its series of annotated booklists are printed in much larger editions than the individual Norwegian libraries could ever afford to, and they are then sold to libraries at a very cheap unit price. In the past, the organization has produced lists on such topics as Africa, Latin America, Race Problems, Sport and Social Problems as well as others devoted to fiction of various types.

The Danish counterpart also produces attractive co-operative publicity, as also does the EKZ in West Germany, and the co-operative library supply agencies in the countries of Eastern Europe.

What of Britain, where no library supply agency exists? The Library Association, and its various groups and sections, has not been inactive in the past. For many years, its County Libraries Section has produced a valuable series of attractive and well-printed *Readers' Guides*, over 120 of them in fact, which public libraries generally have been able to buy cheaply with further reductions for bulk orders. Among these subject lists still in print are those on astronomy, automobile engineering, education, management, photography and numerous other subjects. As long ago as the late 1930s the Association of Assistant Librarians inaugurated a brave venture in the shape of *Recommended Books*, a twelve-page annotated list of general new books which it was imagined would be added to most public libraries. This was attractively printed with a photographic cover, and also contained feature articles on 'Great Books' by various librarian authors. There was a blank space on the front cover so that purchasing libraries could, if they wished, insert the names of their own libraries by overprinting.

Recommended Books was immediately successful and was just becoming accepted by many libraries when the outbreak of war put an end to it. I have always been surprised by the fact that the venture was never recommenced after the war.

In the late 1940s the Library Association itself started producing a series of booklists in folder form on a variety of topics. These listed about 25 to 30 titles with brief annotations and a short introduction, and among the subjects treated were architecture, photography, Georgian England, bird watching, film, personal religion and many others. For some reason or other this activity gradually ceased, but twenty years after the Association again started to produce co-operative booklists, this time fiction bibliographies. More than a dozen of these have already been successfully published in packs of 75 which sell to libraries for £1 each.

√ On the face of it, co-operative library publicity of this kind has much to recommend it. Good quality bibliographies and booklists can be attractively printed and produced at the cheapest possible rates on account of the long print runs, yet many librarians still prefer to produce their own printed lists, often not so attractive and certainly much more expensive in terms of unit cost. The wisest librarians are perhaps those who utilize a combination of both, buying the co-operative products when it suits them to do so, and at the same time exercising their own initiative when it seems more convenient.

Co-operative PR products are of course not confined to printed booklists and bibliographies. Library display kits have been available from both the Library Association in Britain and from central associations and organizations in other countries. These portable and readily assembled kits have been found useful for library stands in careers and other exhibitions.

CHILDREN'S BOOK WEEKS

Children's book weeks have been a feature of library PR work for many years, and examples can be quoted from the United States, the United Kingdom, Scandinavia and indeed many other countries. The earliest instances were those organized by individual libraries, but some countries, notably Denmark, soon began to organize children's book weeks on a national basis. Since I shall be writing about national library and book weeks later in this chapter, only a few general remarks will be made here about the organization of children's book weeks by individual libraries and librarians.

The basic essentials in the planning of a successful children's book week are money, the presence of an energetic and enthusiastic staff, the availability in the library of space for children's events, full co-operation between library and schools, and librarians and school teachers, and finally, an adequate book stock to cope with the increased use which will inevitably follow.

Enough money must be allocated in the budget for a children's book week, to cope with the expenses such as advertising, printing of programmes, speakers' expenses and fees, hire of equipment, transport, prize-giving ceremonies and other incidentals. Unless these have been properly budgeted, it might be advisable not to embark on a children's book week at all. The other salient requirement is close collaboration with local schools and teachers. The advice of the latter should be sought at an early stage with regard to the timing of the book week, which must be for the convenience of the schools and not that of the library. The planning of the programme also needs much care. Children love to meet authors and book illustrators whose names are known to them, but the programme must have variety. As well as talks from celebrities in the world of children's books there ought to be some relevant film shows, puppet shows, and perhaps appearances by sports and TV personalities.

The really important thing is that events should take place in the library, so that the maximum number of children, including non-users, find their way to it and thenceforth know where the library is located. Blatant propaganda should be avoided, but the children's librarian should always, when introducing or thanking speakers, take the opportunity to introduce some encouraging remarks about the facilities offered by the library and how young people can make use of them.

If the children's book week is taking place in a library system with a number of branches it is important to arrange events at each of the libraries so that children and teachers in each locality will not have far to travel and will not feel ignored. It is often quite feasible to arrange for a visiting speaker to appear at one branch in the morning and to give a repeat performance at another branch in the afternoon.

Incidentally, most of the events forming part of a children's book week should take place in school hours, so that school classes can attend the events by prior arrangement with teachers. This is why it is so necessary to time the book week in accordance with the needs of the schools. It is important too, that good notice should be given to the schools of the dates of the book week. In order to ensure that every event is supported by just the right size and type of audience, invitations should be despatched well in advance, care being taken to ensure that, while every seat will be taken, the event is not over-subscribed.

It is not essential to have every event happening in school time, but careful consideration must be given to the planning of evening events. These must be additionally attractive, otherwise disastrously small audiences may result.

The children's book week must be advertised generously, through the press, through posters to be distributed to schools, bookshops, libraries and official notice-boards, and also by the printing of a folder-type programme. This should have an appealing cover to attract young people, and the contents should be in day-to-day diary form, clearly indicating the title of the event, the time, and the name and address of the library where it is to take place. Such programmes must be printed in large editions and distributed to every school in bulk, with additional copies being made available at every library and bookshop in the area.

Copies of the programme should again be sent out in good time, it being a great mistake to leave the distribution too late. Copies will be sent to all local newspaper editors, and to radio and TV editors if appropriate. Editors should be invited to send representatives to all the events, press photographers being especially welcome. The librarian might also arrange to have official photographs taken during the various events of the week, these often being useful for illustrating the subsequent annual report of the library.

Competitions prove to be popular features of children's book weeks, and these may take the form of inviting young people to submit short stories or essays on bookish topics, and perhaps drawings and illustrations for books. The organization of such competitions calls for some thought, particularly the need to have several classes arranged in age groups. Young people ought to be given plenty of time to enter for the competitions, and it is neither necessary nor desirable for entries to be returned during or at the end of the week. A date two or three weeks after the book week is often agreed. Details of the competitions will, of course, be given in the programme and other publicity.

Judging then has to take place, and for this, the librarian is advised to invite teachers to join the children's librarians on the panel. As soon as the results are decided upon, letters should be sent to the successful children, and their teachers should also be informed as a matter of courtesy. Competition prizes usually take the form of books: these are sometimes generously presented by publishers who may have already helped in the arrangements by advising on speakers and providing publicity material. Librarians should not, however, expect to lean too heavily on the goodwill of publishers, and the purchase of book

59

prizes for competitions is a legitimate expense in the organization of the children's book week.

A prize-giving ceremony will then be organized, again at a time suitable to school teachers, and perhaps the Mayor, or a local author or some other celebrity will be invited to present the books. At this ceremony, the librarian will obviously take the opportunity to report on the success of the book week and, since the press will have been invited to send journalists and photographers, extra publicity will be gained from this occasion. A full list of the names and schools of the prize-winners must in any case be sent to the press for publication.

If a book illustration competition has been organized, yet more publicity can be gained from exhibiting the entries at one of the libraries or, better still, in an art gallery or in a prominent shop window. Entries for story or essay competitions can also be used to form part of a children's library magazine.

NATIONAL LIBRARY WEEKS

One of the most ambitious ways of achieving publicity for libraries is by the organization of National Library Weeks. As we know them today, National Library Weeks began in the United States in 1957 and have continued since then up to the present day. Other countries followed suit, notably the United Kingdom, Australia, New Zealand, Canada and elsewhere, but they have tended to be on a more occasional basis than the regular event in America. Much was learnt from early American experience – the need for a national organizing committee including booksellers, publishers and authors as well as librarians, the necessity of having a theme, a symbol, a slogan, and stylized recognizable printed publicity, the need for a book of guidelines and, not least, the basic essential of adequate financial backing. Support for National Library Weeks in the United States, as elsewhere, varies from place to place and indeed from year to year. This is not surprising since library authorities are not always prepared to provide adequate funding every year, while librarians with their limited staffing, cannot regularly participate to the fullest extent that is possible or desirable. Few libraries in the United States support National Library Week every year, but the organization is there for them to utilize whenever they feel they can participate, which for the majority is about once every three years.

BRITISH EXPERIENCE OF NLW

The idea of a National Library Week, or NLW as it is known both in Britain and the USA, was taken up in Britain very soon after it had become established in the United States. The Library Association was the leading protagonist, but some time had to be spent in sounding out opinion in other spheres of the book world, notably the Publishers' Association, the Booksellers' Association and the National Book League. In 1963 dialogues were conducted with the other associations, and in the following year it was agreed to form a Joint Organizing Committee with the intention of producing a National Library Week in the United Kingdom in 1966. Since the present writer was chairman of this NLW Joint Organizing Committee, and remained so until 1969 by which time three National Library Weeks had been organized, the following pages may be of particular interest, the more so since they are written three years later in an atmosphere of detachment.

When the NLW Joint Organizing Committee was formed in the summer of 1964 it was deliberately kept small in membership so that it could act as a kind of executive working party. Originally it was eight in number, with two representatives from the Publishers' Association, two from the Booksellers' Association, one from the National Book League, and three from the Library Association, which was to nominate the chairman. The executive secretaries of the LA, the BA and the PA were included in membership, while the National Book League nominated its director. As time went on it became necessary to widen the membership of the Joint Organizing Committee, which later welcomed representatives of the Society of Authors, the School Library Association, Aslib and the British Federation of Master Printers.

But it was a good idea to keep the JOC down to a small

number at the outset, for there were many matters of detail which had to be decided and for which there was no need for a larger committee. Finance was the first problem to be faced. Neither the LA nor the BA were, or are, affluent bodies, and the NBL had always been largely supported by funds from publishers. So it was to the Publishers' Association that the JOC had to look in the first instance, and to its great credit the PA agreed to contribute the lion's share of the first year's budget.

NLW had many supporters, but it also had many critics. Although the JOC lost no opportunity to tell its critics that more money was needed to ensure the fullest success, it was never fully realized by the outside world that NLW 1 of 1966 was really run on a shoestring. The total budget for the first year, and it was really eighteen months because of the essential preparatory work, was only £10,000. This is a ludicrously small sum by present-day standards, and even in 1965–6 it was only about half what was needed for an event of national significance. Of this £10,000, the PA generously subscribed £7,500, the LA gave £1,500 plus secretarial services and accommodation, and the BA contributed £1,000. Subsequent budgets for NLW 2 in 1967 and NLW 3 in 1969 were even smaller.

It must be emphasized however that much more money was spent on the three National Library Weeks in Britain. Many library authorities allocated special expenditure to them, an untold amount of voluntary effort was contributed, and the associations supporting the Weeks were involved in additional expenditure incapable of being costed exactly.

Once the finance was assured, the first task of the JOC was to appoint organizers for the 1966 NLW. This was done after public advertisement in the summer of 1964. Well over 100 would-be organizers applied and after a short list had been interviewed by the JOC a small firm of PR consultants was appointed. A little-known but very necessary job followed, that of educating the organizers with the elementary politics of the worlds of bookselling, librarianship and publishing, and of acquainting them with the financial limitations of the project.

From then on things moved quickly. They had to because 18 months proved to be not too long a period of preparation for the first National Library Week ever to be held in the United Kingdom. Incidentally there had already been considerable debate on the timing of the week. March 1966 was eventually agreed, though without unanimity. Booksellers and publishers preferred this, but librarians and teachers would have preferred a week in October or November.

It was decided to ask HRH the Duke of Edinburgh to be Patron of National Library Week, and His Royal Highness, whose interest in books and reading is a genuine and deepseated one, readily agreed. It was further agreed to involve as many interests as possible by inviting a number of celebrities to be vice-patrons. The goodwill towards NLW was underlined by the immediate willingness of all those approached to accept these invitations. As a result, the JOC was able to list as vicepatrons such people as the Archbishop of Canterbury, the Secretary of State for Education and Science, the Lord Mayor of London, the Presidents of the Royal Academy, the British Association for the Advancement of Science, the National Union of Students, the National Association of Youth Clubs, and the chairmen of the BBC, the Independent Television Authority, the Arts Council of Great Britain, and the University Grants Committee. The importance of widening the impact of NLW in this way cannot be overestimated.

The JOC and the organizers worked hard in many other directions. After viewing many examples, a symbol was adopted for NLW, also a slogan 'Make time to read'. Royal blue was the chosen colour for all publicity relating to NLW 1, but this was changed to green for NLW 2 in 1967, and to red for NLW 3 in 1969.

It was decided to send the organizers to the United States to study the working and problems of NLW there, and on their return it was agreed that a guide-book should be prepared and published, and that a free copy should be sent to all library authorities, further copies being available for a small fee. This was essentially an 'ideas' book, informing participants of the help and services they could expect from the JOC and the organizers, and also giving them a suggested time-table so that they could prepare for the Week steadily, and keep the organizers informed of their intentions.

63

Discussions were held as to whether the JOC should lay down a theme for the Week, but it was finally agreed not to do this, but to leave it to individual local committees to interpret the Week in the various ways they thought best. I believed at the time that this was the right decision, and on mature reflection I am convinced it was, though some critics thought we should have given a stronger lead here.

Just as the JOC was comprised of librarians, booksellers, and publishers, later to be joined by authors and representatives of education, it was firmly recommended to localities that they should form joint committees at local level, bringing in university professors, teachers, general readers and indeed anyone interested in books. Not all librarians followed this advice, preferring to organize NLW locally through their own efforts and those of their staffs. In many places, especially in small towns and remote localities, the librarians had no alternative. It goes without saying that many dedicated librarians worked miracles on their own initiative in this way, aided by the centralized publicity and guidance which was forthcoming from the JOC and the organizers. But it was also noticeable when the time came to assess the results of the first Week that the most imaginative, comprehensive and successful programmes had emanated from the localities which had operated with wide-based committees.

The centralized publicity material produced by the JOC included not only the guide-book but also crown and double-crown posters, official notepaper capable of being used by any local committee, handbills, bookmarks, car window stickers, envelope stickers, continuous strips for shelves and shop windows, bookmark dispensers and other material. All these items were in blue and carried the NLW symbol, slogan and other information. They were produced in quantities and sold to local committees who benefited from the rates which were considerably cheaper than if they had produced them individually. With the experience of NLW I behind them, the JOC and the organizers produced a kit of the available publicity material for subsequent weeks. These kits were sent out to local librarians with order forms and a request to order early from the organizers.

From the middle of 1965 onwards, the organizers sent out a periodical news-letter to all chief librarians, acquainting them and their local NLW committees with the latest intentions and developments. Local committees were urged to inform the JOC of their intended programmes and many did so. Details of these were printed in later news-letters, and news of this kind was welcomed *pour encourager les autres*. The JOC was sometimes criticized for a lack of communication with those on the perimeter, but this was not an acceptable criticism. The real difficulty experienced by the JOC was in getting enough information of what was happening in the localities. Sometimes it was not until librarians' annual reports were published months after NLW I that the chairman and his committee and organizers learnt that some inspiring and imaginative efforts had been made in many areas. In any future Weeks of this kind it should be borne in mind that communication is a two-way business and that the central organizers fervently want to know of local committees' intended programmes.

One point that needed reiteration was that NLW was not aimed solely at the greater glorification of public libraries. Libraries of all types were urged to participate, and in the end considerable efforts were made by the national libraries, and by some academic and special libraries.

The JOC offered further help to local committees by producing and circulating lists of authors willing to act as speakers, also a list of films available for hiring. The National Book League made its issue of *Guide to Touring Exhibitions* into a special NLW number, and for later weeks it produced some NLW booklists on such topics as *Mainly for women, Africa in the contemporary world, Work and leisure, Growing up with books*, and *Celebrities' choice*. All were available cheaply to local committees. Meanwhile, hundreds of letters were despatched to national organizations explaining the purport of NLW and enlisting support. The Department of Education and Science gave both practical and moral support, as did the local authority associations.

Contact with the press, TV and radio was left to the organizers at national level, though advice was proffered in the handbook urging local committees how best to contact their

c

local newspapers and broadcasting facilities. It proved difficult to project N L W on television, though some success was achieved over the three Weeks. Radio was a much more fruitful medium, and N L W 3 did especially well on the air. All three National Library Weeks had good support from both national and local newspapers, and N L W 2 was well projected by articles in a large number of periodicals. The annual report on N L W 1 printed in the *Library Association Record* of August 1966 mentions that there were 22 radio programmes, and that a total of 868 publications printed over 10,000 column inches on the Week.

N L W 1 was launched nationally with a reception at Guildhall given by the Lord Mayor and the Common Council of the City of London. The National Central Library arranged for its new building to be opened by H M The Queen, who spoke about National Library Week during her opening speech. Foyle's devoted their Literary Luncheon to the Week, many N L W vice-patrons being present. National competitions were arranged by the J O C, mainly for children, though it had been emphasized throughout that N L W was not intended to be merely a children's book week, even though the co-operation of schools and teachers was sought and gained.

The main competition arranged by the J O C was to be judged after the Week itself, and after reports had been received from the 327 local committees which took part. The prize was the Sir Winston Churchill trophy, offered to the local committee which in the opinion of the judges achieved the most imaginative and successful N L W programme. Islington won this for N L W 1, Wakefield for N L W 2, and Cardiganshire for N L W 3.

It is impossible to even begin to list the varied interpretations and activities which took place up and down the country during the Weeks of 1966, 1967 and 1969. Suffice it to say that the collective effort was enormous. The sub-title of N L W 1 was 'A Festival of Books' and many librarians and their committees and staffs displayed great imagination and tireless energy. In addition to the countless displays in shops and libraries, which generally went *en fête*, there were book exhibitions in shop windows, banks, churches, airline offices and elsewhere. Westminster arranged a book display at Madame Tussaud's for N L W 1, and for N L W 3, jointly with Lambeth, had a display of music and gramophone records in one of the foyers of the Royal Festival Hall.

As previously mentioned, local committees were left to interpret National Library Weeks in their own ways. Some interesting variations were noted. Sutton concentrated upon publicizing reference and information work, Cumberland took the opportunity to develop and highlight its service to the housebound, other places chose to focus on children's and school library work, others displayed rare books, and so on.

Novelty was encouraged. It had to be, for despite criticisms from those who deplored such activities as students' processions, beauty competitions and the like, the fact has to be faced that libraries are not sensational news in the eyes of the mass-media. They are just not interested in objective news: lectures and exhibitions in libraries count for nothing in the national press, and for a few lines only in local newspapers. For this reason the organizers were pleased when the students of the NW Polytechnic Library School staged a march with banners in central London. Photographers were on hand, and good publicity was achieved. A similar welcome was given to the idea of the Association of Assistant Librarians to organize a 'Miss Library World' contest for NLW 2, repeated for NLW 3. Here again, publicity was achieved in the national and local press, and especially on TV and radio.

For NLW 2 the Association of London Chief Librarians, backed by the London Boroughs Association, arranged a week-long exhibition devoted to London's public libraries in the concourse of Charing Cross Underground Station. This featured a continuous coloured slide show with expert commentary, an instant reference and information service manned by reference librarians in touch with their libraries by telex and telephone, a stand on librarianship as a career, another stand staffed by children's librarians, a display of library services for special classes of readers, a map of Greater London pinpointing the locations of all public libraries, and stands with book displays on a variety of subjects. The exhibition was visited by thousands of people during the week, among them being the Minister of State in the Department of Education and Science, who met 'Miss Library World' there before the TV cameras.

For NLW 3 a special poem 'In a library' was written by Cecil Day-Lewis, the Poet-Laureate. This was printed in the *Daily Mirror* and later reproduced in *The Library World*. A special number of the *Times Literary Supplement* was issued for NLW 1, and *The Guardian* had a series of articles during NLW 3.

Care was taken not to confine NLW activity to London, and indeed great support was forthcoming from many other cities, towns and counties. Birmingham, Liverpool, Oxford, Luton, Norwich, West Sussex, Leicestershire, Cheshire, Nottingham-shire, North Riding and Cumberland were among the many larger library authorities which featured outstanding NLW programmes over the three years. Even more encouraging was the support which came from many smaller libraries such as York, Chester, Hove, Wakefield, Letchworth and Aberystwyth.

The question is often asked as to what effect the three National Library Weeks of 1966, 1967 and 1969 had, and it is one that is not easy to answer. No one person could possibly appreciate all that was done, and with what success, but the present writer, as chairman of the JOC for five years, is probably in a better position than most. As mentioned earlier, it proved difficult to collect news of everything that was happening, despite the fact that the JOC constantly sought information and also sent out evaluation forms after each of the Weeks. For NLW 1, over 250 evaluation reports were received from local committees, but even this good response left a quarter of the participants unaccounted for.

There can be no doubt that the three National Library Weeks held in the United Kingdom did a great deal to bring libraries and the work of librarians to much wider audiences than ever before. They also helped to improve the images of libraries and librarians by demonstrating a willingness to reach towards the world outside and a readiness to come to terms with modern PR method and meet the requirements of contemporary mass-media. Of course much more could have been achieved, and this will always be the case. There was apathy, even anti-pathy in some quarters, but the disappointment experienced by the JOC was more than cancelled out by the encouragement generated by the many areas which were active and often in-spired by the idea of NLW.

That progress has been made by United Kingdom libraries since 1966 can be proved by comparing statistics of staffing, salaries, book funds, revenue expenditure, loan figures and capital expenditure of that year with those of today. It is not claimed for one moment that NLW's three manifestations are responsible for this progress by themselves. Such forward steps are the results of concerted efforts by librarians, library authorities, the Library Association itself, and the understanding and support of successive Governments. Inflation too, is a factor not to be forgotten. But the idea of National Library Week must be given some credit, helping to keep libraries never far away from the minds, not only of those in the corridors of power, but also in the thoughts of a greater cross-section than ever before of people in general.

If NLW proved worth-while in these ways, why then has it not continued, why was there a gap between 1967 and 1969, and why in 1972 did it re-appear under the new title of National Book Week? These, and other questions, can best be answered by briefly discussing the problems faced by the JOC of 1964 to 1969.

The chief reason why NLW did not become a regular annual event from 1966 onwards was the lack of a regular, dependable and sufficient supply of money. Had this been forthcoming, those responsible for NLW at both national and local level would have been encouraged to carry on, despite other problems. Lack of money was the main reason why there was no NLW in 1968. Because of this, changes had to be made in the national organization and a year's respite was necessary to effect these.

The other main problem was that caused at the perimeter by lack of sufficient library staff. Those librarians who supported NLW 1 to the full with magnificent programmes found it difficult to maintain the momentum for NLW 2. The year came round too quickly for many who had strained might and main with admirable efforts for the first Week. When this became apparent, librarians were circularized and asked whether they would prefer a National Library Week every year, every two years, every three years, less frequently than that, or never. Some brave librarians did opt for every year, and there were those cynics who said never, but the consensus of opinion was for every three years. This useful test of opinion was noted by the new National Book Committee which proposes to organize a National Book Week every three years from November 1972.

It is only fair to mention some of the other difficulties and criticisms faced by the JOC. Some people in the book world complained that the JOC and the organizers appeared to be preaching only to the converted, yet when students' processions, beauty competitions and similar events to titivate the mass-media were supported, other criticisms came in complaining that libraries and books were not being projected with the dignity they deserved. Some librarians refused to support NLW, or did little, because they said their libraries were already being used to the full, and they would not be given extra staff to cope with extra use brought in by NLW. In vain was it pointed out to some of these that NLW was concerned with quality as well as quantity, and that these librarians could have done something by publicizing their rare book possessions, or some of their little-known services appealing only to minorities.

From time to time the JOC heard with a little pain that here and there a lack of collaboration was noticed between librarians, publishers, booksellers and authors. Some mutual recriminations took place. Some publishers thought some librarians were not giving enough support; some librarians complained of inefficiency on the part of some publishers; many librarians were pained by the fact that some authors took advantage of NLW to publicize their demand for a public lending right; and nearly all librarians complained of apathy on the part of booksellers. Yet it must be said that co-operation at national level between the PA, the BA, the LA, the NBL and the Society of Authors could hardly have been bettered, and the individual members of the JOC, though often diverging in their various approaches, made mutual sacrifices and worked together in a way which will always be remembered and appreciated by their chairman. If only the harmony between the different components of the book world which existed at national level could have always been reproduced at the perimeter, and if only more money had been forthcoming on a regular basis, NLW would have been home and dry.

Perhaps the most nagging difference which persisted at national level was the frequent demand by representatives of the Booksellers Association that the title of the event be changed to National Book Week. This was resisted by most librarians and publishers during the five years' existence of the JOC, despite assurances from the representatives of the BA that their members would give more support to an event called National Book Week. After NLW 3 had been assessed, and with the benefit of the results of the questionnaire to librarians, further discussions emanated in the setting-up of a National Book Committee, and the idea of organizing a National Book Week about every three years.

A few librarians, too few to ensure success, are so enamoured of the title National Library Week that they would like to see the LA go it alone, but in the present state of the Association's finances there is no immediate likelihood of this. Many librarians will support a National Book Week and there is no reason why they should not do so. It can offer most of the advantages of co-operative publicity that NLW was able to do. But it remains to be seen whether booksellers will be any more active for NBW than they were for NLW.

OTHER CO-OPERATIVE PUBLICITY

Co-operative publicity for libraries does not have to be national. It can be organized on a regional, county or city basis and there have been good instances both inside and outside the United Kingdom. Book weeks have been arranged within certain counties, involving not only the county libraries but the independent town libraries as well. With the larger library units following local government reorganization in Britain this kind of effort will be facilitated. London librarians could well repeat something on the lines of the Charing Cross Underground exhibition they did for NLW 2. But whenever co-operative library publicity is being planned, librarians should seek help from publishers. They will find this frequently forthcoming in the way of books for display, suggestions and aid in getting authors and illustrators as speakers, and in the provision of much exhibition material, sometimes including authors' original manuscripts and artists' original drawings and paintings.

FRIENDS OF THE LIBRARIES MOVEMENTS

One other method of outreach employed by some librarians is to start a Friends of the Library movement. Usually the chief idea of these is to invite subscriptions later to be used for making special purchases, either books, pictures or *objets d'art*. The chief librarian usually acts as secretary of such a movement, organizes an annual meeting often with a celebrity speaker, and circulates a news-letter to members. In the United Kingdom there is an organization called the Friends of the National Libraries, and another is the Friends of Lambeth Palace Library. There are many examples in the United States and in Scandinavia, notably the Friends of the Malmö City Libraries.

Few public libraries in Britain have embarked in this direction, but it is an idea to be commended for its publicity value. Admittedly only those already converted to books, reading and libraries will actively support such ventures, but the important thing is that such movements do provide additional outlets for publicity. Among the many developments one would hope to see after 1974, when local government reorganization has resulted in fewer but larger public library authorities in Britain, would be a notable increase in Friends of the Libraries Movements.

Chapter 6
Oral library publicity

This chapter deals with the importance of the spoken word as an instrument of library publicity, and it will refer to talks, lectures, discussions, debates and seminars presented both formally and informally to groups of people, both adults and young people. Radio and TV aspects have already been mentioned so we are more concerned here with live talks and presentations.

Before treating in detail the various methods of oral publicity to audiences and groups, it is necessary to say something about the importance of personal oral publicity. By this I mean the more casual and informal approach of telling laymen about the scope, aims, contents and services of libraries through the librarian's private conversation with his friends and acquaintances. It seems to be an occupational characteristic of librarians the world over that they live their jobs throughout practically their whole existence. As a profession we have a reputation for talking shop: some of us may even be bores on the subject and we certainly ought to guard against that. Nevertheless, much good and effective public relations has been done and can be done by librarians taking the opportunity to tell laymen in their private conversations something of the contents and services of their libraries, and to give them a brief inkling of the almost limitless informational and bibliographical work undertaken by their staffs.

In private conversation with chance and business acquaintances the librarian should be an opportunist. He should wait for the inevitable questions which generally come when his profession has been revealed. All experienced librarians will know the sort of naïve questions which come. 'What do you do in a library?' 'Do you have to read all the new books?' – and so on. It is then, and only then, that the librarian should indulge a little quick propaganda on behalf of his calling and of the service he administers. Most people like to hear experts dilating on their subjects, within reason, and this sort of conversational PR can be most effective with the right hearers. Incidentally, it is only when we are talking to the converted that we are in danger of becoming bores on the subject: this kind of PR method, used sparingly and insinuatingly, is capable of bearing the best fruit when directed against the unconverted and perhaps the most unlikely individuals.

TALKING TECHNIQUE

So much for what might paradoxically be called private PR. If we had to rely entirely on this method we should not educate many people about library services in an entire lifetime. Fortunately there are other methods open to us, so we must now turn to the real kernel of this chapter, which is how best to get library and information services over to audiences and groups by oral means. This is a most important aspect of the work of a librarian, for most senior librarians will not have occupied their posts for very long before they receive requests to speak about their work and services to various groups and organizations. If they don't receive such demands, I would hope they would go out and seek opportunities to speak.

Normally however, the public librarian receives many requests to speak about his library – to Rotary Clubs, Round Table Clubs, Chambers of Commerce, businessmen's clubs, literary societies, youth clubs, women's organizations and many others. Likewise, the university and college librarian will be asked and expected to talk about library facilities to intakes of new students, to students' organizations, to members of the faculty, and often to outside bodies as well. The school librarian's time is partly occupied by giving talks and demonstrations to classes, while the special and industrial librarian may also be asked to address senior members of his firm, or groups of staff.

Such opportunities to publicize the library should be seized with alacrity. But what happens if the librarian is a reluctant or ineffective speaker? Obviously the end-product could be disastrous, resulting in bad rather than good publicity for the service. It would appear then that the knack of good public speaking should be part and parcel of the librarian's make-up.

It is difficult to define what makes a good public speaker, but I believe that few are born, more are made. Practice helps enormously, and the aspirant librarian should make it his business to get some public speaking expertise and experience as soon as possible. Textbooks on the subject are helpful, and should be studied, but in the long run there is no substitute for experience. This can be obtained by attending professional meetings, by contributing to discussions, by joining committees both within and outside the profession, and then eventually making one's maiden speech. Many people suffer needlessly from nervous apprehension before addressing audiences and groups of people. They need not do so, for the majority find that their nerves desert them once they are on their feet.

One of the first aims of any public speaker must be to eliminate annoying mannerisms from his delivery. Every speaker, being only human, has mannerisms – some endearing, some annoying – and nobody will be able to eliminate them all. Nor should they try to do this. But some speakers' quirks can be over-annoying to their audiences. Too much walking about, too much shuffling of the feet, too much hand-waving – these are the sort of things which can detract audiences from the really important thoughts the speaker is trying to convey.

Of course the speaker himself is the last person to realize the bad effects of his mannerisms upon his audience, so the question arises of how to detect and eliminate them. One way is for speakers, in their early and tentative days, to plant a friend in the audience, asking him to study the presentation and criticize accordingly. This is perhaps straining friendship a little far, but the speaker should realize that such criticism will be for his own ultimate good. If he has a tendency to shuffle his feet, as so many speakers do, he should be told so. He can remedy this next time by anchoring himself to a lectern, though in a casual rather than a deliberate way. Informality, and lightness of touch, should be retained at all cost.

Inaudibility is an inexcusable sin, and if there is no microphone the speaker should not go wrong if he attempts to throw his voice to the back of the room. The modern tendency, in rooms of any size, is to provide a microphone, and this too can be daunting to the inexperienced. Microphone systems vary in quality, but with a good instrument it should not need more than a sentence or two to come to terms with it. The art is to locate the correct distance between the mouth and the microphone. Most speakers can themselves tell whether they are too close or too far away, and then adjust accordingly. Some speakers, even experienced ones, see a microphone and then say they won't use it, on the grounds that they think themselves capable of being heard everywhere without it. They should think twice about this. Even if they have strong voices capable of being heard on the back row it needs only a bout of coughing in the front rows for those further back to miss the drift of a whole sentence. This results in lack of concentration on the part of many in the audience, and the speaker has to work all the harder to hold their attention. Usually a microphone is provided if thought necessary, so the wise speaker should make use of it.

Some speakers have a fear of drying up, but one who has a good command of his subject ought never to be in this position. Incidentally, the first point any speaker must clear with the organizers of any meeting is how long he is expected to speak. Is it to be twenty, thirty or forty minutes? Will there be questions afterwards, and if so how long should be allowed for these? Quite the best idea is for the speaker to ask the chairman beforehand at what time he aims to close the meeting. Remember that time, work with a watch before you, and bear in mind that the speaker who outstays his welcome will do his cause much more harm than good. Timing is always important, but especially so when addressing businessmen's organizations such as Rotary Clubs. These usually allow only twenty minutes for the speaker, so it is essential to edit one's remarks severely, to intersperse a story or two for light relief, and to leave a little time for questions and answers.

Speaking at too great a length is a very common fault, and it not infrequently happens to the most intelligent speakers, because they have a tendency to be so enthusiastic about their topic that they get carried away and ignore the passing of time. This results in a bored, clock-watching audience who will remember not the content of the talk, but only the fact that the speaker went on far too long. If the speaker happens to be a librarian, then it is the library which suffers from the bad publicity.

Speakers have different ways of disciplining themselves on this problem of length, and of ensuring that they do not dry up prematurely. Some find it necessary to use a prepared script and actually to read this. Usually this is not a good idea, for few people can read to an audience and make the result lively and memorable. Nearly all speakers are much more effective when they are talking to audiences, not reading to them.

The aim therefore should always be to get away from the prepared script. If the speaker still feels the need for a script to fall back on in an emergency, a good idea is to write headings on a small card. This should ensure that the talk will be orderly and well-developed, and that the speaker does not omit the most salient points he wishes to make. He can always fall back on his script on points of detail, or if it is necessary to use a quotation from it.

But there is no doubt that the most impressive and compelling speaker for an audience to listen to is the one who uses neither script nor notes, but who speaks 'off the cuff'. Not only is his delivery more human and natural, he immediately impresses his hearers who can see that here is a speaker who is on top of his subject.

So the eventual aim of all speakers should be to dispense with both script and notes, and to present his talk in the conversational and easy manner which is the only sure way of bridging the gap between speaker and audience. Obviously not everybody is capable of achieving this desirable end, but it should be regarded as the ideal, and many can achieve it gradually by first working from a script, then from notes and script, then from notes only, and finally by casting aside all notes and relying on his memory, his mastery of his subject, and his experience to carry him through.

QUESTIONS AND ANSWERS

It should go without saying that full opportunity should be given for audiences to ask questions of the speaker, and question time should be allowed for in the planning of the talk. The experienced speaker may sometimes deliberately omit one or two signal points from his talk, so that members of his audience may seize upon these and initiate questions with alacrity. On the other hand it sometimes happens that there is an ominous silence when the speaker has sat down and the chairman has invited questions. This should not embarrass the speaker, though it often does, giving him the impression that he has failed in his communication with his listeners. More frequently, it means that he has interested his hearers so much that they have been intent on the talk and have had no time for woolgathering or thinking out possible questions.

Nevertheless, question-time without questions cannot be tolerated, and if an unexpected silence does occur it is the simplest thing in the world for the speaker to revive the session by adding one or two afterthoughts, or even by asking his audience one or two questions and getting them talking in that way.

There is an art too in the answering of questions. It is bad technique, for example, to give what is virtually another talk when answering the very first question. Nothing puts off an audience more than this. People are afraid to ask second or third questions in case they let themselves in for second or third talks. The art, therefore, is to give answers of varying lengths to successive questions. By all means answer in some detail if this cannot be avoided, but redress the balance by responding briefly to some questions. This helps towards greater audience participation, which is surely the objective.

DISCUSSIONS AND SEMINARS

For some time now the trend has been towards more audience

participation, and the popularity of the seminar method of presentation has been increasing. Even if the speaker has been invited to give a full-length talk followed by questions and discussion, the wise speaker will cut down his talk to the minimum and thus extend the time for discussion. But there is an increasing tendency to be invited to address a group on a seminar basis, and since this calls for a different and more difficult technique, special study must be given to it.

Informality is the keynote of the seminar approach. Right from the outset the speaker must create a *rapport* with the group. One way of doing this is to remain sat down, though some speakers find this difficult, preferring to command their audiences from a height by standing up. There is always the half-way house – in other words you can sit on a table or a stool in front of the group.

Contact with small groups of this kind needs to be immediate, and a good way of doing this is to introduce yourself quickly by making some remarks about yourself – your name, your background, your experience, your job. Follow this by introducing some salient points from the topic or standpoint you want to get over, and then, while the group is perhaps not expecting it, toss the ball to them by asking first one, then another member of the audience to describe his or her own background, and to comment on the points you have so far made.

In the context of a library talk this could be done by asking people to tell you what *they* think is the purpose of the library, where they imagine the money comes from for its upkeep, who governs it, what it should or should not contain, do they use it, if not – why not? and so on.

By the time three or four people have made their observations on these lines they will have given the speaker a good idea of the level of his audience, and he can go on to develop his theme before stopping again for further reactions to what he has said. The speaker who is adept at this technique should, before the passing of an hour, have communicated many new ideas about libraries to the minds of most individuals in the group. The time will have sped by quickly, few if any of the audience will have been bored, and most will think that they have made important contributions. Best of all, it is likely that more real knowledge of the library and its service will have been absorbed by the group than if they had listened dumbly to an uninterrupted recital of facts from the lips of the speaker.

VISUAL AND OTHER AIDS

So far we have not mentioned the use of visual and other aids, though talks on the library service lend themselves to their use. In addition to films, film strips, slides and transparencies, speakers can also make use of wall-charts, maps, posters and photographs. More frequently, however, they use films, slides or transparencies, and there are some elementary rules to be observed in the efficient employment of these.

Nothing ruins a speaker's chances of success more than an obvious lack of preparation, so before embarking on a talk with such visual aids as these it is absolutely essential to check on the equipment. The speaker may have his own film or slide projector, but even so he should check on its good working order beforehand. If he is going to use equipment to be provided by the organization he is visiting, then he should arrive early enough to check its efficiency. Elementary matters such as the proximity of the correct electricity supply, the provision of a screen, and the availability of a good black-out should also be verified. With slides or transparencies it is the speaker's own responsibility to ensure beforehand that these are in the correct order and that none will be upside down when they appear on the screen. I did once know a lecturer who purposely put one slide upside down in order to create a laugh and relieve the proceedings. But he was an expert lecturer and a professional. The librarian-speaker would be better advised to avoid this ploy.

Speaking with visual aids calls for a degree of experience and dexterity. A common fault is for speakers to keep some pictures on the screen too long, and then finding that they have to rush the remainder of their slides because time is running short. With visual aids there is no need to stress the obvious. Far

Kom in och låna en bok

The front cover of Stockholm City Library's folder about its children's services is printed in red and black, and beckons children in an appealing way.

know your library

hennepin county library

minneapolis public library

Minneapolis Public Library and Hennepin County Library combine to issue this folder which briefly mentions all services and includes a directory of the thirty-five libraries and five bookmobiles serving the area.

YOUR
SANTA
MONICA
PUBLIC
LIBRARY

1343 Sixth Street
451-5751

SERVICES AND COLLECTIONS....

Santa Monica (California) Public Library's two-fold leaflet can be opened out to form a small poster for bulletin boards.

Few British libraries utilise postcards as PR outlets, but they are common in American and Scandinavian libraries. Here are two examples from Gothenburg City Libraries which speak for themselves. Both are in full colour. In Denmark, the Frederiksberg Public Libraries use picture postcards of the children's library to communicate with their young readers.

Anniversaries offer obvious opportunities for libraries to produce booklists. The Dickens list included a foreword, an illustrated article on 'Dickens and Westminster', and a six-page reading list. The BBC list not only commemorated fifty years of British broadcasting and TV, but was also issued to coincide with National Book Week 1972.

50 years of the BBC

WESTMINSTER CITY LIBRARIES

CHARLES DICKENS 1812–1870

WESTMINSTER CITY LIBRARIES

better to leave something to the audience's collective imagination than to bore the listeners with a description of something they can see for themselves. If an analogy is needed, it is the difference between a good radio commentary and a good TV commentary. The former must be explicit and must set the scene: in the latter, the scene is already set visually and needs only the minimum oral support.

GUIDED TOURS

Some very large libraries, the Library of Congress, the Lenin Library and the British Museum Library among them, have for years been receiving groups of visitors and have found it necessary to employ specialist guides to show these around and to explain the various departments and processes. Many other national, university and large public libraries are now of such size and importance that they too receive many visiting groups, but perhaps not so many as to warrant the employment of specialist guides. These groups are of various kinds: some are comprised of international delegations, others are groups from conferences or from other local authorities, some are groups of students from library schools or other educational institutions, and sometimes they are parties from local schools or societies.

Every individual member of every visiting group will, after his visit to the library, take back with him impressions not only of the building, its contents, staff and services, but also a lasting impression of how the group was received, of how well or otherwise the visit was organized, and of how efficient or otherwise the tour was guided. So it is very important that the director of libraries should devote some careful thought to the planning of such party visits and guided tours.

There should be, and can be, no standardized plan for the reception of visitors who come to tour the library. Everything depends upon the size of the delegation and for what purpose it is coming. There are countless variations. There is the individual professional visitor on a study tour: he or she may not wish to see a conspectus of all departments and processes, but instead may want to concentrate upon one or two aspects of the service. The same may apply to groups of professional visitors. On the other hand, groups of student librarians or those from local schools and societies will probably not want to specialize but to see as much as they can of the service as a whole.

Time is an important factor. Whoever is planning the visit at the library end will want to know how long the individual or group wishes to spend in the library. With this knowledge he can begin to schedule the visit, especially if he also knows whether the tour is to be general in character, or specializing on one or other branch of the service.

Who is to receive the visitor or the party? Ideally, it should be the director of the library, but in large and busy systems receiving many visitors, this is obviously not always possible. Nevertheless, it is always appreciated if the chief librarian receives visitors personally, even if for only a few minutes before passing them on to the staff who will be responsible for the guided tour. I would go so far as to say that it is part of the director's job to receive as many visitors and groups as possible, and to conduct the guided tours as often as he can.

With the best will in the world, the chief librarian cannot possibly welcome all visitors and groups, but when he is prevented from doing so this job should devolve upon his deputy or as senior a librarian as possible. Depending upon the time available, the welcome should comprise a brief talk about the scope of the service, followed by an opportunity for questions from the individual visitor or the delegation. The guided tour should follow this. Whoever is conducting the party can either do all the explaining himself or he can hand over to the head of each section as the tour progresses. If the library is very large and the tour is likely to be protracted, it is perhaps better to allow each section head briefly to explain the work being done by his staff. In this way they get valuable experience in the reception of visitors, and in the art of trimming their explanations to the required length.

Great care should be taken not to tire visitors unduly. Many hosts are naturally enthusiastic about their own services and there is a tendency for them to go on too long. A thought must be given to the creature comforts of visitors: never keep them walking or standing too long, and arrange for them to sit down at the beginning and end of their visit, and in the middle as well if the tour is going to be protracted.

Many large libraries have hospitality allowances, though this excellent arrangement seems more common in American and European countries than it is in Britain. Fortunately, more British librarians are now able to provide some hospitality for visitors, whether it be coffee, sherry or luncheon. This is to be encouraged, for it enables conversations to proceed, and at the same time allows visitors a welcome respite from standing and walking.

At the end of the visit the opportunity should be taken to present visitors with a portfolio of the library's PR material, including the latest annual report, printed booklists, and folders outlining the services. Any offprints of articles relating to the service might also be included. It is important to make this and any other presentations at the end of the visit and not at the outset. If the visitor or party is from overseas an offer to send on the portfolio is sometimes appreciated. On the other hand, some visitors prefer to take them away personally.

This point about presenting PR material after the visit is over also applies to talks and lectures. Never present handouts before a talk, always at the end. Audiences with handfuls of PR material on their knees have a tendency to let their attention waver. On the other hand, if the speaker sees his visitors taking notes and vainly trying to copy down facts and figures he should tell them that they will be given PR and other material at the close of the proceedings.

Chapter 7
Exhibitions, display work and other activities

Libraries, with their books, music, gramophone records and tapes, archives, maps, prints, drawings and a host of other materials, have great potentiality for audio-visual appeal, and this can be expressed through exhibitions, displays, concerts, lectures, film shows and in other ways. As with all other PR activity these can be put on well or badly, the difference being that the end result will create either an impressive or a discouraging image for the library. Amateurism is the bogey many libraries have suffered from in the past, not perhaps so much in the organization of lectures, poetry, readings, concerts and film shows, but more especially in the conduct and presentation of visual displays and exhibitions. In this chapter we shall examine how best to project library services in all these ways.

INSIDE AND OUTSIDE THE LIBRARY

The best exhibition a librarian can ever hope to put on is his own library building and its contents. Fortunate is he who has a recently constructed building, for if the planning has been imaginative he should have a well-sited library in the modern idiom of design, a building which has the come-hither look, and one which openly displays both by day and by night that here is a library. The first steps will indeed have been taken to attract users to it.

Many new libraries, and some old ones for that matter, have shop-window type frontages, eminently suitable for displays, and illuminated so that passers-by after dark will be attracted to them. It is quite essential that shop-window displays in libraries are colourful and attractive, also that they are changed

84

frequently and do not contain any out-of-date material. The librarian-in-charge would do well to get into the habit of looking at the windows every morning to check that they are good advertisements for the library. More will be said later about the problems of maintaining good displays in library windows.

Inside the building, the library should be in a constant state of display. The foyer should be large and welcoming, with a well-staffed information desk in the foreground, a few display cases – also frequently changed, by the way – to appeal to browsers with a few moments to spare, and bulletin boards containing posters and notices neatly displayed. A daily check on these is also essential for nothing parades faulty and inefficient organization more than bulletin boards flying tatty and out-of-date notices.

The shelving in the library should be of contemporary design, with adequate guiding in clear lettering. Amateur efforts at guiding should not be tolerated and if any temporary guiding is necessary, as it sometimes is with a new building or after a re-modelling of the interior, it should be replaced as soon as possible with more permanent arrangements. Display fitments can with ingenuity be introduced into the shelving plan: these help to break up long runs of shelving and offer opportunities to present small displays of a topical character. The PR aspect of the physical presentation of the library should be completed with the book stock itself, which should be live and up-to-date, clean and colourful.

The majority of library displays take place in the library, or perhaps in its foyer or shop windows. A vast amount of work goes into the preparation of such exhibits, which do much to draw attention to the contents of the library to those who already use it, but does little or nothing to attract non-users. It was one of the valid criticisms of much National Library Week activity that many librarians confined their preaching to those already converted, and a similar censure can be levelled at a lot of library display activity.

The library should be more outreaching. More exhibitions and displays should be arranged outside the confines of the building.

It is surprising what can be achieved with outside bodies if goodwill and initiative are employed. Department stores can sometimes be persuaded to admit a library display into one of their windows, and smaller shops too will often co-operate, perhaps not so much with a large exhibit, but certainly they will sometimes welcome a mini-display with a library motif. Hotel lobbies, airline offices, the foyers of business offices, railway and bus stations, academies and schools can all be thought of in this connection. The city or town hall foyer should not be forgotten, and local church halls and village halls can often be used.

Any place where people pass, visit, meet or congregate in their daily lives should be considered suitable for a library display, and co-operation should be sought to produce one.

The next consideration is what to exhibit. New books, rare books, manuscripts, prints, illustrations, photographs, music and other library contents are the norms, supported by well-designed posters and notices drawing more blatant attention to the library. The advantages to be gained from introducing artefacts and non-library materials are not always appreciated, but they are real advantages. A display of books on sport can be brought to life by such shop-window dressing as the introduction of a football, a golf club, a tennis racquet, a skate or a cricket score-card. A window show of books on costume and dressmaking could be easily augmented by models, dress materials and the like; an exhibition of books on police and the law might be backed by a pair of handcuffs, a truncheon, and some 'Wanted' posters from the past; a show of literature on science can easily be enlivened with some chemical apparatus and portraits of such people as Pasteur and Fleming; an exhibition of music will be made more attractive by the judicious display of various musical instruments. The reader is left to produce his own additional examples. The possibilities are endless.

Many such artefacts can often be produced by members of the library staff, whose help should always be encouraged. But people and organizations from outside the library will often lend their possessions quite willingly if they are approached. A source which librarians often ignore are foreign embassies and consulates, which invariably help if asked by producing posters, photographs, booklets, leaflets and other material relating to their countries. Airlines and travel agents are similarly helpful in augmenting book displays relating to different regions or various countries of the world. A model aircraft or train or other kind of transport, with some coloured posters and some objects indigenous to a country will catch passing eyes much more than an unsupported display of books.

The presentation of any library display or exhibition will be made or marred according to whether it has a professional or an amateur look about it. An increasing number of libraries now employ professional display artists, and we have already seen how useful these members of staff can be in helping to design printed publicity. But it is in the conception of book displays that the library artist comes into his own. With guidance from the professional librarians he can create a recognizable style of library posters and notices, and he should in fact work very closely with librarians-in-charge to create effective displays and exhibits. Experience has shown that once a professional commercial artist has been added to the library personnel it is not long before another, and another, is needed.

If the library is of such a size that a full-time commercial artist cannot be justified, consideration should be given to employing a part-time one if possible. Failing this, the librarian should not hesitate to enlist the aid of an outside commercial firm of experts in design and display, especially if his display is part of a larger exhibition in which other interests are on show. This often happens, at agricultural shows, local government exhibitions, careers and 'Welcome to citizenship' exhibitions, and the librarian must keep up with the Joneses. He cannot afford the library exhibit to be compared badly with other stands. Amateurish design and poster-writing can never hope to match professional effort, and is never a good advertisement for the service it is trying to sell.

Official openings, with the resultant press and photographic coverage, should be aimed at when the library is organizing a major exhibition of its own services. These require careful organization to ensure that the ceremony passes off without a hitch and that maximum PR coverage is attained. Choice of opener is important: a university library may invite the

Vice-Chancellor or an eminent professor, a school library might aim for somebody prominent in the world of education, a public library may ask the Mayor or the chairman of the appropriate committee. These are obvious choices, but it has to be said that more publicity will be obtained if the opener is a TV or show-business personality, or even a well-known author.

Exhibition openings must be planned well in advance, so that not only can the guest speaker be booked, but also arrangements made to ensure the presence of an audience, and the best possible coverage by the press, radio and TV. The whole object of having an official opening must be to publicize the exhibition, and it is fatal to fall down on the PR aspects. An audience may be invited through letters to selected people, or better still an attractively printed invitation card will be sent. It is nearly always safe to send out more invitations than there are seats, because not all those invited will be able to attend. For short opening ceremonies, especially of exhibitions, seats are not always provided, and as people take up less space when they are standing it is additionally safe to despatch many more invitations than accommodation would apparently warrant. It is much better to have a press of people present rather than a sparse audience.

Editors should receive details in good time, so that they may make arrangements for journalists and photographers to be present, and this applies to editors of topical TV and radio programmes as well. Every facility should be made available to the press, and since the chief librarian will be busy with his official guests, another senior librarian should be made responsible for receiving representatives of the press and other media. He should be capable of answering all their questions both before and after the opening ceremony.

Photographs are of prime importance. Cameramen who are covering the ceremony for their editors will take such pictures as they think most appropriate, but it is essential that the librarian should think of his own requirements, and it may be necessary for the library to employ a photographer to take the kind of pictures wanted for posterity, and for use in annual reports and film strips, or as slides to accompany future PR talks. Many library exhibitions have been ingenious in their design, full of colour and attraction, and well worthy of permanent record. But they are not on show for ever, and many a librarian has regretted not having photographs or slides of a display or exhibition he was once proud of, but which has sadly been dismantled before the need for a pictorial record was envisaged.

LECTURES, CONCERTS AND OTHER ACTIVITIES

So far in this chapter we have dealt with visual outreach, but there are many other ways of promoting the library through what used to be called extension work. Fortunately in recent years it has become an accepted fact that libraries should involve themselves with general cultural activities. It is no longer true to describe this involvement as 'extension' work since it is part and parcel of libraries' programmes.

The organization of lectures, concerts, recitals, film shows, play and poetry readings is difficult if the library building does not contain an auditorium or hall suitable for the purpose. So many older library buildings still in use do not have this provision, but their librarians have skilfully contrived to present this type of activity, even though it has meant using the children's room or some other part of the library after closing time. Of course this is never fully satisfactory, but it is better than nothing, and it shows willing. It can in fact be a useful pointer in persuading governing bodies that the building is inadequate for the purpose of interpreting modern librarianship, and thus indicating the need for a new, purpose-built library, properly equipped for the housing of books and other material and for the library to take its rightful place in the cultural life of the community.

Whether a library contains a theatre, an auditorium, a series of halls, or merely one all-purpose and flexible hall, depends on many factors, chief among which are its size, location and purpose. It was in the United States that librarians first grasped the need for the library to include facilities of this kind, and many examples may be seen there, both in older buildings and in recent erections. I myself have seen excellent provision in such places as Minneapolis, Santa Monica, Akron and elsewhere. Following closely upon American example, the Scandinavians have also been to the fore in including theatres, auditoria, and halls for community use in their splendid new libraries. Gothenburg's city library, opened in 1967, features a comfortable theatre with stage and dressing rooms, with fixed seating for 196 people, and facilities for the projection of films and slides. One of many uses made of this auditorium is by a group of actors from the city theatre, who put on performances of plays by arrangement with the Library authority.

Solna and Eskilstuna in Sweden, Lyngby-Tårbaek and Randers in Denmark, Kuopio and Rovaniemi in Finland are just a few of the many places in Scandinavia where recent library planning has included enviable space for a wide range of cultural events. There are also examples to be found, though not yet enough, in Germany, Czechoslovakia, Hungary, Romania and other countries.

In the United Kingdom there is still a long way to go before it can be said that all libraries are properly equipped in this direction. Nevertheless, a number of library authorities have shown the way. Manchester, where the central library was planned in the late 1920s and opened in 1934, displayed great foresight by the inclusion of a library theatre which has proved its worth many times over since then. At first intended as an auditorium for lectures and meetings, it began to be utilized as a theatre *per se*, and productions have continued almost uninterruptedly, bringing the library to the forefront of people's minds.

In more recent years there is increased evidence that British librarians and library authorities have taken the hint. Public libraries built in the 1960s at Holborn, Luton, Eastbourne, Bradford, Grimsby, Epsom and other places have made good provision for cultural events. Luton, profiting from Scandinavian experience, included a theatre with fixed seating for 240 people, with a stage, two dressing rooms and projection room. Holborn provided an adaptable hall with a stage and an exhibition foyer. Even more ambitious was Bradford, where the new city library houses a 400-seat theatre with good cloakroom and refreshment facilities adjacent. Cafés and snack-bars in libraries are relatively recent features on this side of the

Atlantic, but happily they are increasing in number and no doubt will become even more common in future. If cultural events are to be pursued in the library, creature comforts such as adequate toilet and cloakroom space, as well as refreshment possibilities are essential. Apart from anything else, they are good for public relations.

Camden's latest library in Euston Road includes the Shaw Theatre where members of the National Youth Theatre present regular productions. This is a splendid auditorium with fixed banked seating, a generous stage and dressing rooms: altogether a great attraction in an already appealing and inviting library. In Epsom and Ewell there is a striking new building, circular in shape, which was opened in 1970 and goes far in the direction of being the complete social and community centre for residents. As well as exhibition space and a local history museum, it houses facilities for concerts, conferences, lectures, film shows, amateur dramatics, dances, receptions, parties and meetings of all kinds. There is also a separate suite of rooms for adult education purposes. This social accommodation includes a main hall seating 360 persons, a large stage and projection room, and in addition there is a smaller hall seating 110, a banqueting room accommodating over 200 diners, a large kitchen and an anteroom. The banqueting room can be divided into three segments for use as small meeting rooms when not required for its prime purpose. It should be mentioned that at Epsom the social accommodation is not the responsibility of the librarian, but the fact that it is housed in the library building is a great publicity asset for the library service.

Westminster's new district library in Paddington, now in course of erection, will include over 500 square metres of space devoted to cultural and artistic pursuits. There will be a large exhibition hall, plus four other rooms at maximum, although these can be converted into larger rooms if desired. Thus at any one time the library could be presenting an art exhibition, a film show, country dancing, story-telling or a lecture.

There are a number of points to be borne in mind when planning libraries with cultural accommodation. The most important is that the latter should be accessible when the

library is closed, so there must be separate entrances, stair-
cases, lifts, cloakrooms and toilets. Wiring for stereophonic
sound should also be considered, so that record recitals can be
presented. Projection facilities must be allowed for, while any
halls or foyers designed for exhibition use should have picture
hanging facilities discreetly built into the walls. If the cultural
accommodation is not on the ground floor, lifts must be provided to help the handicapped and the aged to have access to
the areas where the events are taking place.

INTERNATIONAL ENCOURAGEMENT

In the recently revised IFLA Standards for Public Libraries
there are numerous references to the public library's duty to
act as a cultural centre for its community. Since the original
Standards published in 1958 were almost completely silent on
this point, this is an indication, if one were needed, of the
strides which have been taken in the interim to link public
libraries with wider cultural activities and interests. The revised Standards incorporate the UNESCO Public Library Manifesto as a preamble and, after averring that 'the public library
is concerned with the communication of information and ideas,
whatever the form in which these may be expressed', the Manifesto goes on to say: 'The public library is a natural cultural
centre for the community, bringing together as it does people
of similar interests. Space and equipment are therefore necessary for exhibitions, discussions, lectures, musical performances and films, both for adults and children.' The UNESCO
Manifesto adds: 'The public library should be active and positive in its outlook, demonstrating the value of its services and
encouraging their use. It should link itself with other educational, social and cultural institutions, including schools, adult
education groups, leisure activity groups and with those concerned with the promotion of the arts.'

Such a positive statement from an agency of such universal
standing as UNESCO needs no underlining.

The revised IFLA Standards themselves give great prominence to the need for public libraries to help and indeed initiate

cultural events in the community. Paragraphs 42 to 48 are concerned with audio-visual materials in the library, and without such materials and equipment the library will be handicapped from the outset in its cultural objectives.

Paragraph 80 is so definite as to require quoting in full. It says: '. . . there will often be advantage in linking the public library with other community services such as exhibition halls and theatres. In certain circumstances it may even be possible for a public library to serve simultaneously as the library of a school or other educational institution, especially when that institution aims to meet more comprehensively the cultural and social needs of the community. By such means as these the community will often be able to gain the maximum use and value from a number of related facilities'.

In the later revised Standards which deal specifically with public library buildings, guidance is given on the need for adequate space for storing AV materials and equipment, and paragraphs 98 to 100 draw attention to the necessary space and installations for their utilization. Paragraph 108 refers to accommodation for activities in children's libraries, and the subsequent paragraph deals with exhibition space in public libraries stating that 'Every public library should provide opportunities for exhibitions . . . as an extension of its educational, cultural and informational functions.'

As a preamble to the revised IFLA Standards, some general principles are enunciated, based on the UNESCO Manifesto. One of these utters a perhaps necessary word of warning, and this must be quoted in full. It says: 'Despite the recognized importance of the public library in cultural and educational development, it must, if it is to fulfil its purposes, maintain its separate identity, and remain an independent institution. This need in no way hamper the library's sponsorship and encouragement of cultural projects, nor prevent association at a local level with community organizations, social education, or literacy promoting organizations, particularly in developing countries'.

All those who have seen examples of the public library being relegated in importance by inclusion in huge palaces of culture will realize the necessity of this warning, and will take heed of it.

Let us therefore take every opportunity, both when planning our library buildings and when developing our services, to further cultural activity through lectures, discussions, displays, exhibitions, concerts and in other ways, and certainly let us extract the maximum P R value from these events. But never let us forget that the library is the basis of our extensions in these directions.

Chapter 8
The future of library promotion

Public relations are a form of communication, and the problem of communication is one of the most difficult that besets management in all its fields of activity. No matter how meticulous are the arrangements for the transmission of information from the decision-maker to his staff, there will always be complaints of a break-down in communication. Far from deterring management in its efforts, such complaints should be used as the basis for improvement.

It must not be forgotten, however, that communication is a two-way business. If the librarian and his staff are to work effectively as a team, and they must, arrangements must be made not only for the librarian to keep his personnel fully informed as to his intentions, but also for the prompt and regular feed-back of information from the senior staff to himself. Many library directors have brilliant ideas for new developments, which they implement, but then they forget all about the necessity of inquiring into the progress and effects of these ideas, because they are either too busy with yet more ideas or, more likely, they have not arranged for adequate feed-back.

Methods of communication between librarians and their staffs have already been mentioned, and it will be recalled that these include regular staff meetings as well as news-letters initiated by the decision-maker. Many business organizations produce house journals to aid communication between management and staff, but only the very largest libraries will be able to use this method. Nevertheless, as library systems grow in size, library directors will be forced to consider all possible means of keeping large, diversified and far-flung staffs informed of plans and developments. Feed-back is more difficult to organize, but it can and must be arranged. More prominence should perhaps be given in staff meetings to feed-back from section heads to the librarian, rather than the Olympian distribution of information from the top. But to make this effective it must not be forgotten that section heads must also arrange for their own feed-back from the working librarians in their sections.

THE VALUE OF COURSES

There are now many short courses available on management, on computer applications, on programmed budgeting, and on other modern techniques impinging upon library administration. There have also been short courses on public relations from time to time, but not nearly enough of them, and probably librarians have not sufficiently supported those which have been arranged. Librarians should without doubt take more advantage of attending such courses themselves, or of sending their senior staff to them. Library associations, for their part, could be more active in helping to initiate short courses or even one-day study conferences in conjunction with institutes of public relations.

Whoever attends such courses from the library should be asked either to circulate summaries to other senior members of the staff, or else to give a brief account of what he has learnt to a meeting of senior librarians. In this way the knowledge and expertise gleaned from the course can be spread more widely, and more librarians will become more PR conscious.

In future, library schools throughout the world must devote more of their curricula to public relations for librarians. This is not to say that some library schools, especially in the United States and Britain, do not already cover this important topic, but they do not appear to give it the same prominence as they do to other aspects of management. More thought might be given to inviting visiting lecturers from the PR field to address student librarians in the schools, while the schools themselves could do much to encourage interest in the subject by arranging displays of library publicity, and by organizing short study conferences open to practising librarians as well as to their own students.

PUBLICITY FOR SPECIAL SERVICES

I believe that in the past librarians have tended to devote too much time and expense to general publicity and not enough to their special services. With the accent on more specialization more attention will have to be devoted to publicizing those special activities of libraries which appeal to smaller, self-contained audiences. When we think of the special services and collections which more and more libraries are developing – the growth of audio-visual services, work with young adults, housebound services, special collections for the non-indigenous population, books for slow readers, books for the partially-sighted, and the growth of special collections consequent upon the development of subject specialization schemes – all these in addition to such traditional services as those to children and schools, to research students, to local historians, and to commerce and industry, make it imperative that the library publicity of the future should be more specifically produced and distributed.

This means the production of fewer general catalogues, booklists and folders in favour of many more special lists and promotional material. It also means the compilation and maintenance of more specialized mailing lists. Local directories can be used for this purpose, but every ingenuity needs to be employed, and suggestions from the library staff should be encouraged and welcomed. Liaison might be sought with the secretaries of local associations and groups so that, for example, publicity for the local history and archives collection might be beamed to all members of local amenities associations, and not merely to their secretaries or chairmen.

In the same way promotional material concerning services for the housebound, the blind, the partially-sighted and other handicapped people should be circulated to all doctors, ministers of religion, welfare workers, old people's clubs and charitable groups in the community. Members of tenants' associations should also be sent any material concerning library services to children, young adults and elderly and handicapped people. Business houses and commercial organizations and offices

D

remain strangely ignorant of what the library can do for them, and a really determined effort should be made by librarians in the future to achieve better communications with the world of business. Closer contacts must also be sought with the members of literary, artistic and scientific societies in connection with the issue of publicity describing library holdings in these fields.

The permutations of this type of mini-circularization are almost limitless, and it would be idle to pretend that every effort of this kind will result in impressive gains, quantitatively speaking. But the combined results of many such mailings will undoubtedly pay off, because they will reveal to a large number of specialists the undisputed fact that the contemporary library is not so much a mass of general literature as a collection of special libraries, and that the librarian and his staff, which includes an expanding element of subject specialists, are aiming to satisfy the book and documentary needs of specialists in the world of today.

DIRECT ADVERTISING

No references have yet been made to direct advertising, because this is something that few libraries have tried, except when they have been advertising for staff, or announcing lectures, recitals, concerts, exhibitions or similar cultural activities. This situation may well have to change in the future and indeed, since libraries have a duty to inform the public of their services, I see no reason, except perhaps the fiscal one, why they should not indulge in direct advertising from time to time in newspapers and magazines, on commercial radio and TV, and on hoardings, buses, underground railways, theatre and concert programmes – anywhere, in fact, where the public eye may be caught.

Because libraries are a public service there has been a tendency to try to get our publicity on the cheap through press releases and the like. Of course, direct advertising is not cheap and it is becoming more expensive as time goes by, but if a large library were to publicize its services this way for an experimental period the results would certainly be closely watched by colleagues everywhere.

A few libraries have used direct advertising by having posters printed for display on official notice boards, but these have often been little more than a directory of the names, addresses and telephone numbers of the libraries in a system, with perhaps a few headlines pinpointing the main services given. Even this is better than nothing, though efforts should be made to display such posters on a much wider basis than on official notice boards, and outside and inside the library buildings themselves.

Poster advertising should be developed much more. A series of posters should be prepared, each one emphasizing a special facet of the library service. They should be arresting in their colour and design, which means that the services of professional commercial artists should be employed. The possibilities of co-operation should be examined here, and library associations and library service agencies could perhaps advance this idea more positively.

Such library posters as one has seen in the past have always tended to be too general, and certainly they have tried to say too much. Direct advertising, whether it is to be a box advertisement in a newspaper, a large poster for use on hoardings, a smaller advertisement on a bus or on a railway station, must be eye-catching, and must also carry messages which are curt and compelling.

LIBRARY SURVEYS

Another commercial practice to which more librarians should resort in future is to discover, by means of marketing surveys, who uses the services and for what reasons, and who does not use the service, and why they do not. If they do use the service, or one part of it, are they satisfied, and have they any suggestions to make for its improvement?

Reading surveys are nothing new, and many examples can be quoted which have taken place at national, regional and local level. But such surveys have been very sporadic, and few have been carried out with contemporary expertise. The conduct of marketing surveys is now a highly sophisticated and specialized technique, calling for professional advice and organization. In Britain, the Booksellers' Association is to be commended for having a bookshop survey conducted by Dr Peter Mann of the University of Sheffield. Is it not time that the Library Association, and indeed library associations in other countries, prompted similar surveys on the use of libraries?

A number of individual librarians have already issued questionnaires to their readers, or to a proportion of them, but one sometimes wonders how expertly the questionnaire was phrased, what the librarian was trying to prove, and what – if anything – happened when the results had been collated. In any event, such questionnaires are reaching only those who already use the service, and while the observations of such people are important and can sometimes lead to improvements, we are surely more concerned with the large numbers of people who, for one reason or another, do not utilize libraries.

To be of maximum value, library surveys call for careful pre-planning. First, the objects must be defined. Is it intended to discover why people do not use libraries? Or, if they do, how they use them? Or is it to be aimed at a small group of users of a special collection or service? Is it to be a mere sampling, or is the coverage to be as comprehensive as possible? These, and other questions, need consideration at the outset.

If the survey is to be carried out by means of a questionnaire, its type and wording warrant great care. Questions need to be kept as brief and explicit as possible, and they should ideally be of the kind that can be quickly answered by ticks in boxes alongside. Few people mind responding to a questionnaire which they can see at a glance can be dealt with quickly, but they will demur at lengthy, complicated questions which appear to call for detailed answers. The purpose of the survey should be succinctly stated at the top of the paper: this much at least is owed to the respondents. Unless absolutely necessary, people should not be asked to give their names, but in any case it ought to be made clear that strict anonymity will be preserved in any publication of the results. At the end of the form the opportunity should be afforded for people to write any general observations or comments they may wish to make.

The distribution of the survey forms is the next consideration. If the survey is to concentrate upon existing users, say of a reference library, the forms can be handed out to readers by the staff personally, or they can be left on desks in the hope that users will complete them and return them to the staff on the way out. If, on the other hand, the survey is to be more outreaching, more problems are posed in the issue of the questionnaire forms. The librarian may decide to concentrate upon a certain district, in which case he might mail a copy to every resident in the area, using the electoral registration lists as guides. Sent through the post in this way, it will be essential to include a brief and polite letter, asking for co-operation, not forgetting to enclose a reply paid envelope for the return of the form.

Another and more economical way of distributing questionnaires through the post is to use a sampling method, sending them out say to every fifth or every tenth name in a directory or an electoral list. It is essential not to make the sampling too sparse, because experience shows that surveyors are lucky if they receive back more than a quarter of the forms despatched. When it comes to collating the forms, nothing can be more misleading than a small number of returns.

Instead of mailing the questionnaire forms, the librarian might prefer to take a leaf out of the book of the public opinion polls, and employ people to stop passers-by on the streets, asking for quick responses to a small number of questions. Many pedestrians are not too happy about being interrupted in this way, but others will go out of their way to be interviewed. Obviously the questions have to be few, brief and quickly answerable. It might make an interesting feature of some future book week to have a library employ a few students, or even members of its own staff, in such a pavement survey.

But however the survey is done, the cardinal values of it come out in the collation of the answers. This needs to be done with great accuracy, and the results should be published in one form or another. They should prove useful to many other librarians as well as to the one who has initiated the survey.

The survey report can form a good public relations document in itself: but more than that, it can offer a solid foundation for any future PR policy.

To sum up, I want to see librarians of the future becoming more PR conscious, and more expertise in using PR techniques. They must secure higher budgets for promotional activities, and they must not be afraid to follow commercial practices by using good print, attractive colours, house symbols, direct mail, direct advertising, special beamings, house journals, on-the-spot opinion polls and the hundred and one other methods of the advertising and communications businesses.

Libraries have something of great value to offer to the community. It is a crime not to say so, and to keep on saying so, by all the means at the disposal of librarians.

Select bibliography

COPLAN, Kate. *Effective Library Exhibits.* New York, Oceana Publications. 1958.

DOVE, Jack. 'Librarians and Local Radio'. *Assistant Librarian,* 64: 6, June 1971, p. 86 *et seq.*

ELLIOTT, C. A. *Library Publicity and Service.* London, Grafton. 1951.

HARRIS, W. B. 'Public Relations for Public Libraries'. *Assistant Librarian,* 64: 2, February 1971, pp. 18–19.

HOLMAN, William R. *Library Publications.* San Francisco, Roger Beacham. 1965.

NATIONAL Library Week 1966 Annual Report. *Library Association Record,* 68: 8, August 1966, pp. 284–8.

RABURN, J. 'Public Relations for a Special Public'. *Special Libraries,* 60, December 1969, pp. 647–50.

RENBORG, Greta. 'Library Public Relations'. Anglo-Scandinavian Conference on Public Libraries, Sjusjøen, Norway, 1964. Pp. 52–9. Oslo, Statens Bibliotektilsyn.

RENBORG, Greta. 'Public Relations Activities for the Stockholm City Library'. *Scandinavian Public Library Quarterly,* 3: 1, 1970, pp. 1–13.

ROBERTS, R. G. 'Public Relations in Libraries'. *British librarianship and information science, 1966–1970,* pp. 581–9. London, The Library Association, 1972.

SHERMAN, S. B. *ABCs of Library Promotion.* New York, Scarecrow Press. 1971.

TERLAND, Helge. 'Contact and Information Activities in Public Libraries'. Anglo-Scandinavian Conference on Public Libraries, Koli, Finland, 1970. Pp. 42–58. Helsinki, Finnish Library Association.

Index

Index

Advertising, 98–99
All-Union State Library for Foreign Literature, Moscow, 37
American Library Association, 11, 54–55
Annual reports, 32–34
Articles, magazine, 46–48
Aslib, 61
Association of Assistant Librarians, 31, 56, 67
Association of London Chief Librarians, 67
Auditoria, 89–94

Biblioteksentralen, 55
Bibliotekstjänst, 55
Booklists, 35–36, 56–57
Booksellers' Association, 61, 62, 70, 71, 100
Bradford Public Libraries, 90
British Council, 13
British Federation of Master Printers, 61
Bulletins, library, 34

Camden Public Libraries, 91
Catalogues, 34
Chairmen, committee, 17
Cheshire County Libraries, 21, 52
Children's Book Weeks, 57–60
Committees, library, 16

Commonwealth Library Association, 13
Communications, staff, 20–21
Competitions, 59–60
Computer typesetting, 38–39
Concerts, 89–92
Co-operative publicity, 54–72
Courses, 96
Cultural activities, 89–94

Dana Awards, 31–32
Day-Lewis, Cecil, 68
Denmark, 55
Department of Education and Science, 14
Discussions, 78–80
Displays, 84–94
Distribution of publicity, 39–40
Duplicator, use of, 38–39

Edinburgh, HRH Duke of, 63
Education, 18
Exhibitions, 84–94

Féderation Internationale de Documentation, 11–12
Films, 53
Foyle's Bookshop, 66
Friends of Libraries, 72

Index

Gothenburg Public Libraries, 90
Guided tours, 81–83

Holman, William R., 30, 39

IFLA, 11–12, 92–94

Lambeth Public Libraries, 66–67
Lectures, 89–92
Letter-writing, 27–28
Library Association, 11–12, 56–57, 61, 100
Library Association Record, 66
Library publications (Holman), 30
Library World, 32, 68

Magazine articles, 46–48
Malmö City Libraries, 72
Mann, Peter, 100

National Book League, 61, 62, 65, 70
National Library Week, 18, 46, 60–71
Newspaper stories, 46–48
North Riding County Libraries, 21
Notepaper, 26–27
Norway, 55

Oral publicity, 73–83

Parliament, 14–15
Personal service, 23–29

Photographs, 43–45, 47
Powell, Lawrence Clark, 30, 31
Press conferences, 44–45
Press releases, 42–44
Printing, 30–40
Public Lending Right, 15, 70
Public relations librarians, 21–22
Public relations officers, 21–22, 48–49
Public speaking, 74–78
Publishers' Association, 61, 62, 70

Radio, 50–52
Recommended Books, 56
Renborg, Greta, 21
Report writing, 16–17
Rules and regulations, 25–26
Rylands, George, 17

Scandinavian Public Library Quarterly, 21
School Library Association, 61
Seattle Public Libraries, 22
Seminars, 78–80
Service leaflets, 36–38
Snaith, Stanley, 31
Society of Authors, 61, 70
Special services, 97–98
Stationery, 28–29
Stewart, J. D., 32
Stockholm City Libraries, 21, 37, 38
Surveys, library, 99–102
Sweden, 55

Telephone, use of, 26
Television, 50–53
Times Literary Supplement, 68
Toledo Public Libraries, 21

Toronto Public Libraries, 33

Unesco, 11–12, 92–93

Visitors, 81–83

Visual aids, 80–81

Westminster City Libraries, 66, 67, 91
Writers' and Artists' Year Book, 47